Learning Google Apps Script

Customize and automate Google Applications using Apps Script

Ramalingam Ganapathy

BIRMINGHAM - MUMBAI

Learning Google Apps Script

First published: March 2016

Production reference: 1140316

Published by Packt Publishing Ltd.
Livery Place
35 Livery Street
Birmingham B3 2PB, UK.

ISBN 978-1-78588-251-7

www.packtpub.com

Credits

Author
Ramalingam Ganapathy

Reviewer
Serge Gabet

Commissioning Editor
Priya Singh

Acquisition Editors
Vinay Argekar

Pratik Shah

Content Development Editor
Sachin Karnani

Technical Editor
Prajakta Mhatre

Copy Editor
Charlotte Carneiro

Project Coordinator
Neha Bhatnagar

Proofreader
Safis Editing

Indexer
Rekha Nair

Graphics
Abhinash Sahu

Production Coordinator
Aparna Bhagat

Cover Work
Aparna Bhagat

About the Author

Ramalingam Ganapathy is an independent computer software professional with more than 15 years of working experience of JavaScript and Google Apps Script. In 1985, he started his career as a digital electronic circuit designer and service engineer. Highly interested in reading technical books and building electronic projects, he is a detail-oriented and logical person. Since 2001, he has been freelancing with Elance and Upwork (formerly oDesk). He earned a good reputation on the Upwork portal, and most of his clients are satisfied.

> I must thank and dedicate this book to my wife, Thiripurasundari, who served me coffee late at night. Also my son, Muhilan, and daughter, Rajalakshmi, who tested the code from the beginner's point of view.

About the Reviewer

Serge Gabet has been a professional audio equipment manufacturer for 20 years and is now working for an artistic upper school in Brussels, Belgium, as a teacher and technical manager. He is also in charge of the Google Apps administration of this school. He develops custom applications using Google Apps Script mainly for his school, though he also works in other areas.

He has been designated a top contributor by Google since June 2011. He was active on the Google Group Help forum until 2012, then on the Stack Overflow forum (the Google Help Group forum was closed in June 2012), and became a first ranker and an all-time contributor on the Stack Overflow forum a few months ago.

I'd like to thank all the forum contributors who were on the same forum at the time that I was new to the forum and helped me take my first steps. Most of them are now top contributors too, and even if their knowledge was (and still is) greater than mine, they never make me feel it. Thanks for that.

Also, thanks to Google collaborators for their day-to-day presence and for listening to our concerns.

www.PacktPub.com

eBooks, discount offers, and more

Did you know that Packt offers eBook versions of every book published, with PDF and ePub files available? You can upgrade to the eBook version at www.PacktPub.com and as a print book customer, you are entitled to a discount on the eBook copy. Get in touch with us at customercare@packtpub.com for more details.

At www.PacktPub.com, you can also read a collection of free technical articles, sign up for a range of free newsletters and receive exclusive discounts and offers on Packt books and eBooks.

https://www2.packtpub.com/books/subscription/packtlib

Do you need instant solutions to your IT questions? PacktLib is Packt's online digital book library. Here, you can search, access, and read Packt's entire library of books.

Why subscribe?

- Fully searchable across every book published by Packt
- Copy and paste, print, and bookmark content
- On demand and accessible via a web browser

Table of Contents

Preface

Google Apps is a collection of applications, namely, Gmail, Calendar, Drive, Docs, Sheets, and Forms. You can customize or automate Google Apps using the scripting language JavaScript with Google's defined classes. Google implements Google Apps Script (GAS) based on JavaScript.

Almost all Google Apps provide one or more services. GAS services and APIs provide easy access to automate tasks across Google products and third-party services. You can use these service classes in your GAS code to customize or automate Google Apps.

This book introduces basic things first before moving to advanced concepts step by step with practical code and examples. By reading this book, you'll gather expertise in Google Apps Script. Happy reading!

What this book covers

Chapter 1, *Introducing Google Apps Scripts*, tells you about Google Apps and gives you an introduction to Apps Scripts, explains how to create a project, and introduces custom formulas.

Chapter 2, *Creating Basic Elements*, covers many types of dialog and how to create and display them, how to use the Logger class to log values, and how to debug your script.

Chapter 3, *Parsing and Sending E-mails*, talks about the ContactApp, MailApp, and GmailApp services. Using these services, you'll create many useful real-world applications, including an e-mail merger application.

Chapter 4, *Creating Interactive Forms*, deals with creating Forms dynamically by script, publishing the script as a web application, creating Forms using HtmlService, creating an e-voting application, and creating a ticket reservation application.

Chapter 5, Creating Google Calendar and Drive Applications, teaches the reader to create Calendar events and sync events from one Calendar to another Calendar. This chapter also teaches how to enable GAS advanced services.

Chapter 6, Creating Feed Reader and Translator Applications, is about learning and creating many useful applications, including RSS/Atom reader and language translator applications.

Chapter 7, Creating Interactive Webpages, tells how to create an RSS feed/publisher, a file uploading application, and a full-blown timesheet application using HtmlService.

Chapter 8, Building a Workflow Application, explains how to create a workflow application and proceeds create a useful real-world order processing application.

Chapter 9, More Tips and Tricks and Creating an Add-on, is all about using external libraries including OAuth2, and Apps Script add-ons.

What you need for this book

You will need any modern browser and basic working or theoretical knowledge of HTML, CSS, and JavaScript.

Who this book is for

This book is for newbies to Google Apps Script who have less practical experience of web development and curious to gather expertise in customizing Google Apps and developing web apps.

Conventions

In this book, you will find a number of text styles that distinguish between different kinds of information. Here are some examples of these styles and an explanation of their meaning.

Code words in text, database table names, folder names, filenames, file extensions, pathnames, dummy URLs, user input, and Twitter handles are shown as follows: "A default myFunction function will be there in the editor."

A block of code is set as follows:

```
function greeting() {
  Browser
}
```

When we wish to draw your attention to a particular part of a code block, the relevant lines or items are set in bold:

```
</head>
<body>
  <button onclick="alert('Hello World!');">Click Me</button>
</body>
</html>
```

New terms and **important words** are shown in bold. Words that you see on the screen, for example, in menus or dialog boxes, appear in the text like this: "Go to **Add-ons | Chapter 2 | Show Dialog** and a modal dialog will pop up."

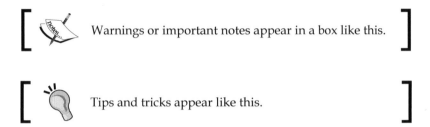

> Warnings or important notes appear in a box like this.

> Tips and tricks appear like this.

Reader feedback

Feedback from our readers is always welcome. Let us know what you think about this book—what you liked or disliked. Reader feedback is important for us as it helps us develop titles that you will really get the most out of.

To send us general feedback, simply e-mail feedback@packtpub.com, and mention the book's title in the subject of your message.

If there is a topic that you have expertise in and you are interested in either writing or contributing to a book, see our author guide at www.packtpub.com/authors.

Customer support

Now that you are the proud owner of a Packt book, we have a number of things to help you to get the most from your purchase.

Downloading the example code

You can download the example code files for this book from your account at
`http://www.packtpub.com`. If you purchased this book elsewhere, you can visit
`http://www.packtpub.com/support` and register to have the files e-mailed
directly to you.

You can download the code files by following these steps:

1. Log in or register to our website using your e-mail address and password.
2. Hover the mouse pointer on the **SUPPORT** tab at the top.
3. Click on **Code Downloads & Errata**.
4. Enter the name of the book in the **Search** box.
5. Select the book for which you're looking to download the code files.
6. Choose from the drop-down menu where you purchased this book from.
7. Click on **Code Download**.

Once the file is downloaded, please make sure that you unzip or extract the folder
using the latest version of:

- WinRAR / 7-Zip for Windows
- Zipeg / iZip / UnRarX for Mac
- 7-Zip / PeaZip for Linux

Errata

Although we have taken every care to ensure the accuracy of our content, mistakes
do happen. If you find a mistake in one of our books—maybe a mistake in the text or
the code—we would be grateful if you could report this to us. By doing so, you can
save other readers from frustration and help us improve subsequent versions of this
book. If you find any errata, please report them by visiting `http://www.packtpub.`
`com/submit-errata`, selecting your book, clicking on the **Errata Submission Form**
link, and entering the details of your errata. Once your errata are verified, your
submission will be accepted and the errata will be uploaded to our website or added
to any list of existing errata under the Errata section of that title.

To view the previously submitted errata, go to `https://www.packtpub.com/books/`
`content/support` and enter the name of the book in the search field. The required
information will appear under the **Errata** section.

Piracy

Piracy of copyrighted material on the Internet is an ongoing problem across all media. At Packt, we take the protection of our copyright and licenses very seriously. If you come across any illegal copies of our works in any form on the Internet, please provide us with the location address or website name immediately so that we can pursue a remedy.

Please contact us at copyright@packtpub.com with a link to the suspected pirated material.

We appreciate your help in protecting our authors and our ability to bring you valuable content.

Questions

If you have a problem with any aspect of this book, you can contact us at questions@packtpub.com, and we will do our best to address the problem.

1

Introducing Google Apps Scripts

I know there may not be a single person in the world who has access to the Internet who has not used at least one of Google's products or services in their lifetime.

Google is known for its famous search engine, the video serving portal YouTube, and now by its numerous web applications, namely Gmail, Calendar, Drive, Docs, Sheets, and Forms. It also provides cloud computing and other software services.

The word "Google" has even become a verb, referring to conducting a web search. Nowadays, you hear people saying "I Googled something" rather than "I searched the web for something". In this chapter, you will learn about Google Applications, Application Scripts, and how to create a custom formula/function.

Google Applications

Google Applications are a collection of applications, namely Gmail, Calendar, Drive, Docs, Sheets, and Forms. From now on, we will use the term "Google Apps" or just "Apps".

Before we start, I'll quickly answer a few questions you may have:

- Where do all these Apps run? On your computer?

  No, all these Apps run on Google's Cloud-based servers.

- How can you get access to these applications?

    You can interact with these Apps through web browsers. No special hardware or software installations are required except for a modern web browser installed on your desktop, laptop, tablet, or smartphone.

Google Apps Script

You can customize or automate Google Apps using the JavaScript scripting language with Google-defined classes, known as **Google Apps Script (GAS)**. Google implements GAS based on JavaScript 1.6 with some portions of 1.7 and 1.8. The GAS services and APIs provide easy access so users can automate tasks across Google products and third-party services.

You can write code in Google Docs, Sheets, and Forms using GAS and can automate tasks similar to what Visual Basic for Applications does in Microsoft Office. However, GAS runs on Google's server and the results are rendered in your browser. The integrated script editor allows you to edit and debug your scripts within your browser, and you do need not install anything. You can activate your debugged and tested script functions to run either based on your interactions or based on a trigger in response to an event or timed intervals (in minutes, hours, days, weeks, future dates, and so on). These events include onOpen, onEdit, onInstall, and many more. GAS is also used to create add-ons for Docs, Sheets, and Forms.

GAS can help you with every aspect of automating a task—you can even use it to order a pizza at predetermined date/time!

Visual Basic for Applications

Microsoft implements **Visual Basic for Applications (VBA)** to help automate Office applications such as Excel and Word. For each respective application, VBA is known as Excel VBA or Word VBA and so on. Using Excel VBA, you can create macros for Excel known as "Excel macros". GAS is for Google Applications, and operates in the same way as VBA does for Microsoft Office applications. Although both VBA and GAS do not require a separate compilation process, they are very different scripting languages and use different programming APIs, methods, and properties.

I hope many of you are familiar with using VBA for Office applications; if not, then never mind—that's not an obstacle to learning GAS.

The advantages of GAS over VBA

- **Version-independence**: Sheets/Docs along with scripts are automatically saved in the cloud, attached to your Google account, and accessible from any computer with a browser. There is no need to worry whether the other computer has the same version of Sheets/Docs installed or not, whereas we can never be sure that one version of the Excel/Word macros will work on another version.

- **Platform-independence**: When you create VBA macros in Excel/Word on the Windows platform, they may not work on the Mac platform and vice versa. With Google Sheets/Docs, it doesn't matter what platform you're working on—it'll work.

The limitations of GAS

GAS runs on Google's server, so it cannot run continuously for more than six minutes (this may vary in the future). All of your functions should finish running and should return results within this time limit. Don't panic, as you'll learn how to use triggers effectively to overcome these limitations later.

In the following sections, we will take a look at the most popular Google Apps and how we can use GAS to customize and/or automate tasks.

Google Drive

Google Drive is a file storage application, which from now on we will just refer to as "Drive", where you can store and synchronize your files on Google's server. Let's look at some of the advantages of using Drive:

- You can edit and share Google Docs, Sheets, and Forms with your friends or collaborators in real time.

- You can even stop editing a document on one of your desktops and continue with your smartphone or tablet, and vice versa, no matter where you are and what device you are using. This is possible because your files are stored on Google's Cloud server.

- Files created with Google Apps are stored in Drive with Google's native formats and extensions. For example, Google Docs (documents) files are .gdoc, Google Sheets (spreadsheets) are .gsheet, and so on.

- In addition to Google's native files, you can also store or upload any other type of file from your desktop to Google Drive.

 If you would like to synchronize files on your computer or devices with Drive, then you can install special software called **Google Drive Client Application**. While this application is running on your computer or device, it synchronizes files stored locally with the same files in Drive.

You may be wondering, what is the purpose of synchronizing files? Sometimes you may need to, or someone may ask you to, parse a CSV file stored on a desktop using GAS to process the data and organize it into a Sheet. In this case, GAS won't execute on the desktop, but it can on the Google server. This way you can access your Drive files and parse data within your synchronized CSV file. You don't have to upload the CSV file manually every time to Drive.

The following screenshot shows the Drive folder view:

Gmail

Gmail is the most popular web-based e-mail service and is provided by Google. With it, occasionally composing and sending e-mail messages manually to one or a few people is not a problem. But what if you want to send an e-mail at a predefined time when you are not awake or to multiple recipients? Consider the following scenarios:

- You want to send a surprise birthday greeting to your friend at a fixed time; neither earlier nor later
- You need to send customized e-mails to hundreds of people at a time

- You need to send e-mails periodically

For all these scenarios, GAS has the answers:

- Using GAS, you can build a mail merger application to send e-mails with customized greetings or messages to *n* number of people.
- You can extract information buried in e-mails from your inbox and store and organize them in Google Sheets or Docs.
- You can even convert the data or contents of a Google Sheet or Docs to a PDF or any other file format and send it as an e-mail attachment, or just save the created file in Drive and include only the file's URL as a hyperlink in e-mail messages.
- In addition, GAS also allows you to mark selected messages as important, or starred. You can also add, delete, and update your Gmail Contacts using the Contacts service.

The following screenshot shows how Gmail classifies or groups messages with labels:

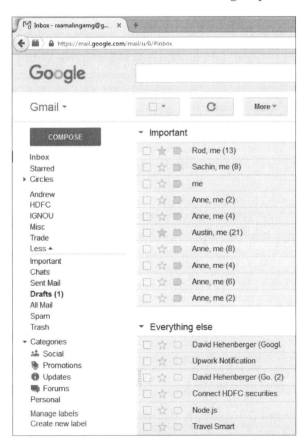

Google Calendar

Google's online Calendar service is integrated with Gmail. GAS provides access to Calendar service by using the `CalendarApp` class. Using GAS code, you can access and modify your Calendar and those you have subscribed to. Using GAS, you can create Calendar events and invite your friends programmatically. Alternatively, you can grab event details and populate them in Sheets.

Google Docs

Google Docs is a word processing program, and runs on web-based software within the Google Drive service. Docs allows you to create and edit documents online while collaborating with other users in real time. Using GAS, you can create documents, format the contents, translate them to other language, save them in Drive, or e-mail them to your friends.

Google Sheets

Google Sheets is a spreadsheet program much like Microsoft Excel. You can create Sheets, share them with others, and edit them in real time. Google provides built-in formulae/functions in Sheets. You can also create your own simple to complex formulae. In other words, you can create custom formulae. Using the `SpreadsheetApp` class in your GAS code, you can interact with other applications.

Google Apps services

Google provides Apps services to enable GAS to interact with the Apps. Almost all of the Apps provide one or more services. You can use these service classes in your GAS code to customize or automate Apps. Services are grouped as **basic** and **advanced**. You can use basic services directly, but for advanced services you need to enable them before using them. You will see how to enable them later on.

Creating Google Sheets in Drive and sharing them with your friends and the public

Here are the steps to create a Google Sheet:

1. Run your favorite browser and type `https://drive.google.com/` in the address bar.

 In order to use Google Drive, you should have a Google account. If you don't have an account, then create one.

2. Now the Google Drive page will open. In the left pane, click on the **NEW** button and on **Google Sheets**:

3. After creating a new Sheet, right-click on it (Windows) or context click (Mac) and select the **Share...** option:

4. A new pop-up window will open as shown in the following screenshot. After that, enter the e-mail address, or addresses, with which you would like to share the document. Finally, click on the **Done** button:

Google will send a share notification to your friend(s). When your friend(s) click on the access link provided, they will get access to your document.

Congratulations! You have created a new Sheet and successfully shared it with your friend(s).

Script projects

Scripts are organized as projects. Projects can be of two types, standalone and bounded to a gtype (Google Drive native file type, such as Sheets, Docs, and Forms) file. Standalone scripts are created in a separate script file, you can see these files listed among other files in Drive. Bounded scripts are embedded within individual gtype files and created using the respective applications. As you can see, the standalone script files, among other files in Drive, you can open directly from Drive, but bounded script can be opened within respective applications only. However, bounded script will have more privileges over parent file than standalone scripts. For example, you can get access to the active document within bounded scripts, but not within standalone scripts.

Creating standalone script projects

To create a standalone script file follow these steps:

1. Follow the steps as described in the *Creating Google Sheets in Drive and sharing them with your friends and the public* section.

2. Navigate to **NEW | More | Google Apps Script** rather than the spreadsheet, as shown in the following screenshot:

3. A new untitled project will open in a new browser tab or window. The new project includes one code file, Code.gs, with a blank function, myFunction, as shown in the following screenshot:

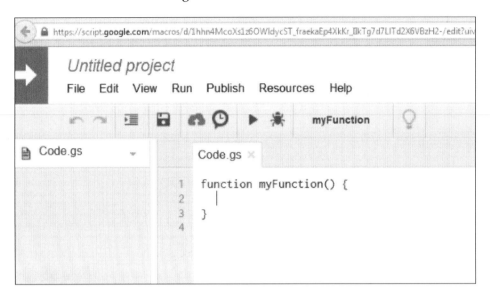

4. To save or rename the new project, press *Ctrl + S* on your keyboard or click on the **Save** icon (floppy disk) in the editor. If you are saving the project for the first time then a prompt will appear to enter a new project name. Enter the project name (whatever you like) and click on the **OK** button. The new script file will be saved in the current folder:

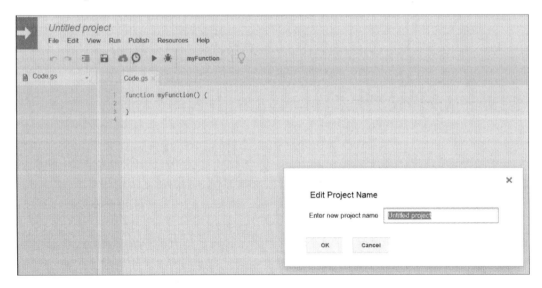

Creating new projects in Sheets

Create a new Sheet or open the existing one. You will see a number of menu items at the top of the window. Now, follow these steps:

1. Click on **Tools** and select **Script editor...**, as shown in the following screenshot:

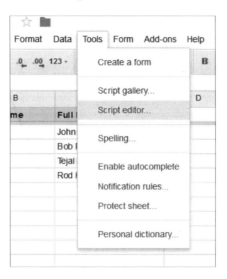

2. A new browser tab or window with a new project selection dialog will appear, as shown in the following screenshot:

3. Click on **Blank Project** or close the dialog (you do not need to always select **Blank Project**, just this time). A new untitled project will open in a new browser tab/window.

4. Save the project as described in the preceding section.

 Although you can create as many bounded projects as you like, one project per file is enough. Creating just one project per file may help you to avoid problems with duplicate function and variable names.

Congratulations! You have created a new script project. By following the preceding steps you can create script projects in Docs and Forms too.

Creating a custom formula in Sheets

Open the spreadsheet you created earlier and make the following changes:

1. In columns *A* and *B*, type a few first and last names.

2. In cell *C2*, type (including the equals sign) =CONCATENATE(A2," ", B2).

Now you can see the first name and last name in cells *A2* and *B2* respectively, concatenated with a space in between.

CONCATENATE is Google Sheet's built-in formula. You can also create your own, called custom formula:

1. Open the script editor and copy-paste this code:

```
function myFunction(s1,s2) {
    return s1 + " " + s2;
}
```

Here is the screenshot for the same:

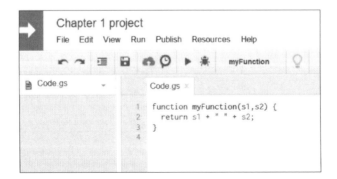

2. Press *Ctrl + S* on your keyboard or click on the **Save** icon in the editor to save the script.

3. Now return to the spreadsheet, and in cell *C2*, type `=myFunction(A2,B2)`.

   This works in exactly the same way as the built-in formula. You can extend your formula to other cells below *C2*. This is a simple formula, but you can create complex formulae as per your requirements.

4. Your custom formula should return a single value or a two-dimensional array. The following screenshot shows how a custom function will work:

	A	B	C	
	fx	=myFunction(A2,B2)		
1	First Name	Last Name	Full Name	
2	John	Doe	John Doe	
3	Bob	Peter	Bob Peter	
4	Tejal	Patel	Tejal Patel	
5	Rod	Holder	Rod Holder	
6				

Congratulations! You have created a custom formula.

To add code completion and/or tooltips for your custom function, add the following comments at the preceding lines of code in the function:

```
/**
 * Concatenates two strings
 *
 * @customfunction
 */
function myFunction(s1,s2){
    ...
```

Google Forms

Google Forms is a Google App that you can use to collect information from your users. User responses or answers are collected and stored as responses in the Form itself and then can be populated in the connected Sheet. You can also change the response's target Sheet when required. You can create Google Forms dynamically using GAS.

Creating Forms within Google Sheet

In the spreadsheet you created earlier, click on the **Tools** menu and select the **Create a form** option. A new Form will be created and is bound to a new Sheet automatically. The new Sheet's name will be similar to `Form Responses 1`. In the new Form, create form fields with headings exactly same as in the Sheet's column headers:

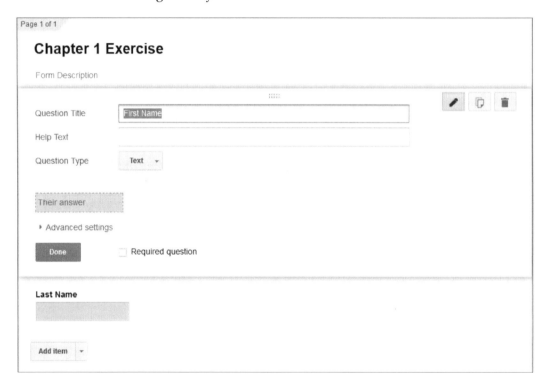

On completion, try submitting the data using a live Form.

Some research

If you are given a document's ID or key, something like `11CEeHWygGKqxGS7jmQzLpeO7Fs3cjetT4HTrWXHTDSU`, can you open the document, provided it has been shared with the public?

 Every Google Doc, Sheet, folder, and project has an ID or key, which you can get from the corresponding item's URL.

Summary

In this chapter, you learned about Google Apps and got an introduction to GAS, as well as how to create a project and custom formulas. There are many more Google Apps available but we just covered the most popular ones. It will not be hard to adopt the same scripting concepts and principles for other Apps. In the next chapter, you will learn to create basic elements such as custom menus, dialogs, and sidebars.

2

Creating Basic Elements

In the previous chapter, you learned about **Google Apps Script (GAS)** and how to create a script project. In this chapter, you will learn how to create a clickable button, a custom menu, a message box, a sidebar and dialogs, as well as how to debug your script. We will use Sheets for the first two tasks and Docs for all the other tasks.

Creating a clickable button

In the previous chapter, you learned how to open the script editor in Google Sheets. For this task, open the script editor in a newly created or any existing Google Sheet and follow these steps:

1. Select cell *B3* or any other cell. Click on **Insert** and select **Drawing...**, as shown in the following screenshot:

2. A drawing editor window will open. Click on the **Text box** icon and then click anywhere within the canvas area. Type Click Me. Resize the object to enclose the text only, as shown in the following screenshot:

3. Click on **Save & Close** to exit the drawing editor. Now, the **Click Me** image will be inserted into the active cell (*B3*), as shown in the following screenshot:

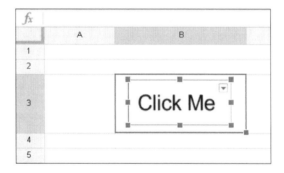

You can drag this image anywhere around the spreadsheet except in the menu bar.

In Google Sheets, images are not anchored to a particular cell, and they can be dragged or moved around.

If you click on the image, a drop-down arrow on the top-right corner will be visible:

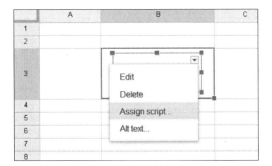

4. Click on the **Assign script...** menu item. A script assignment window will open. Type greeting or any other name you like, but remember the name as the same name will be used to create a function in the next steps. Click on **OK**:

5. Now open the script editor in the same spreadsheet. When you open the script editor, a project selector dialog will open. You can close it or select **Blank Project**. A default function, myFunction, will be there in the editor. Delete everything in the editor and insert the following code:

```
function greeting() {
  Browser
}
```

When you type . next to `Browser`, the code completion hint will open as shown:

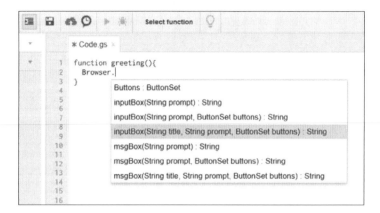

If you click on `msgBox(String title, String prompt, ButtonSet buttons):String`, then `msgBox(title, prompt, buttons)` will be inserted automatically.

In addition to the code hint feature, you can use the auto-indent feature. Ensure that the **Indent** icon, on the left side of the **Save** icon, is pressed. Select the few lines of code you would like to indent, then press the *Tab* key on your keyboard. Now you can see that these lines of code indented automatically.

In this code, `Browser` denotes that you are calling the `Browser` class from the `Base` (or basic) script services. `msgBox` is the `Browser` class's method with three parameters. The names of the parameters are self-explanatory. The `title` parameter denotes the title of the message box, `prompt` denotes your message to the user, and `buttons` denotes what category or sets of buttons you would like to include in your message box.

6. Now edit or replace the code with the following:

```
function greeting() {
  Browser.msgBox("Greeting", "Hello World!",
    Browser.Buttons.OK);
}
```

7. Click on the **Save** icon and enter a project name if asked. You have completed the coding of your `greeting` function.

8. Now, activate the spreadsheet tab/window and click on your **Click Me** button. An authorization window will open and you need to click **Continue**. In the successive **Request for Permission** window, click on **Allow**, as shown in the following screenshot:

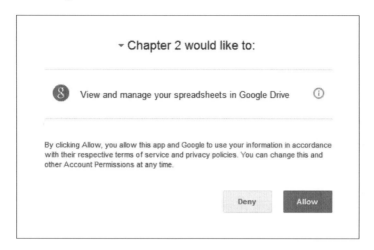

You only need to do this once for this particular scope. The scopes will be shown in the concerned permission dialog/window. In this script, the scope is **View and manage your spreadsheets in Google Drive**. Above the scope, you can see the title **Chapter 2 would like to:**, which means your script project (project name **Chapter 2**) or application would like to get your permission for that particular scope.

As soon as you click **Allow**, the permission dialog will close, and your actual greeting message box will open as shown here:

Click **Ok** to close the message box. Whenever you click on your button, this message box will open.

Congratulations! You have created a clickable button and associated a GAS function with it.

Showing toast when a button is clicked

Toast appears as a popup window in the lower-right corner of the active spreadsheet with a title and message. To create a toast dialog, edit or replace the greeting function as follows:

```
function greeting() {
  SpreadsheetApp.getActiveSpreadsheet()
    .toast("Hello World!", "Greeting");
}
```

Now if you click the button, then a toast dialog will appear as shown in the following screenshot, and it disappears within 5 seconds (the default):

You can include a third argument, that is, timeout seconds, in the toast method. This means how long the toast will be visible for. Put a negative number if you want it to show up forever. For example, toast("Hello World!", "Greeting", -1).

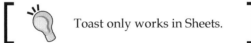

Toast only works in Sheets.

Creating a custom menu

You might be wondering whether you can execute the greeting function without the help of the button. The answer is yes. In the script editor, there is a **Run** menu. If you click on **Run | greeting**, then the greeting function will be executed and the message box will open.

Creating a button for every function may not be feasible. Although you cannot alter or add items to the application's standard menu (except the **Add-ons** menu) such as **File**, **Edit**, **View**, and so on, you can add custom menus and menu items.

For this task, create a new Google Docs document or open an existing document. Open the script editor and type these two functions:

```
function createMenu() {
  DocumentApp.getUi()
    .createMenu("PACKT")
    .addItem("Greeting","greeting")
    .addToUi();
}

function greeting() {
  var ui = DocumentApp.getUi();
  ui.alert("Greeting", "Hello World!", ui.ButtonSet.OK);
}
```

In the first function, you are using the DocumentApp class, invoking the getUi method, and consecutively invoking the createMenu, addItem, and addToUi methods by method chaining. The second function should be familiar to you, as you created it in the previous task, but this time with the DocumentApp class and associated methods.

> Do not copy-paste these functions or codes; create/edit them yourself line by line. This will help you become familiar with the script editor's code hinting and completion features.

Now run the createMenu function and flip to the document window/tab. You will see a new menu item called **PACKT** added next to the **Help** menu. You can see the custom menu **PACKT** with an item **Greeting** as shown in the following screenshot. The item label **Greeting** is associated with the function greeting.

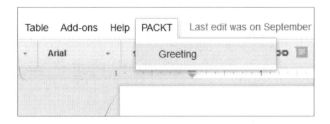

The menu item **Greeting** works the same way as the button created in the previous task. The drawback with this method of inserting the custom menu is that to get the custom menu to show up, you need to run `createMenu` every time within the script editor. Consider how your user would be able to use this `greeting` function if they didn't know about GAS and the script editor. Think about how your user may not be a programmer like you. To enable your users to execute selected GAS functions, you should create a custom menu and make it visible as soon as the document opens. To do so, rename the `createMenu` function `onOpen`, and that's all.

> The `onOpen` function is a special function name. Whenever a user opens a document, the GAS interpreter executes this function first. Other similar function names are `onEdit`, `onInstall`, `doGet`, and `doPost`. The first two are spreadsheet event-related functions and the next two are published script service's `get` and `post` callback functions. You should not use these function names other than for the intended purposes.

Creating a sidebar

A sidebar is a static dialog box and is included on the right-hand side of the document editor window. To create a sidebar, type the following code in the editor:

```
function onOpen() {
  var htmlOutput = HtmlService
  .createHtmlOutput('<button onclick="alert(\'Hello
    World!\');">Click Me</button>')
  .setTitle('My Sidebar');

  DocumentApp.getUi().showSidebar(htmlOutput);
}
```

In the preceding code, you are using `HtmlService` and invoking its method `createHtmlOutput` then consecutively invoking the `setTitle` method. To test this code, run the `onOpen` function or reload the document. The sidebar will open in the right-hand side of the document window as shown in the following screenshot. The sidebar layout size is a fixed one, which means you cannot change, alter, or resize it.

The button in the sidebar is an HTML element, not a GAS element, and if clicked, it opens the browser interface's alert box.

Creating an Add-ons menu

In the previous task, you included the HTML code inline as a string argument to the createHtmlOutput method. Alternatively, you can put this HTML snippet in a separate HTML file.

To create a new HTML file, in the script editor, go to **File** | **New** | **Html file**, as shown in the following screenshot:

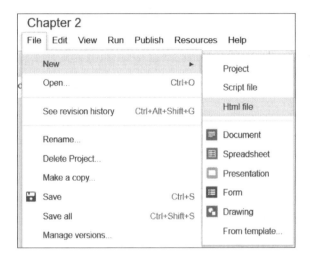

Then in the **Create File** box, enter your preferred name for the new HTML file. For this task, enter Index and click on the **OK** button. The .html extension will be added automatically.

A new `Index.html` file will be created with a few lines of default HTML code, as shown in the following screenshot:

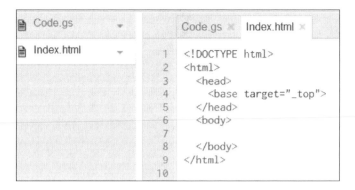

Insert your `button` tags between the `body` tags as shown here:

```
<!DOCTYPE html>
<html>
  <head>
    <base target="_top">
  </head>
  <body>
    <button onclick="alert('Hello World!');">Click Me</button>
  </body>
</html>
```

Insert the code shown here in the `Code.gs` file:

```
function onOpen(){
  DocumentApp.getUi()
  .createAddonMenu()
  .addItem("Show Sidebar", "showSidebar")
  .addToUi();
}


function showSidebar() {
  DocumentApp.getUi()
  .showSidebar(
    HtmlService.createHtmlOutputFromFile('Index')
    .setTitle('Greetings')
  );
}
```

To test the code, run the onOpen function or reload the document. In the **Add-ons** menu, a new item, called **Chapter 2** (the project name), will be added, as shown here:

Show Sidebar is the label for the showSidebar function; click on it to show your sidebar.

Creating a modal dialog

To create a modal dialog, which prevents the user from updating anything in the spreadsheet or document, update the code in the Code.gs file as shown here:

```
function onOpen(){
  DocumentApp.getUi()
  .createAddonMenu()
  .addItem("Show Dialog", "showDialog")
  .addToUi();
}

function showDialog() {
  var html = HtmlService
    .createHtmlOutputFromFile('Index');
  DocumentApp.getUi()
    .showModalDialog(html, 'Greeting');
}
```

Go to **Add-ons** | **Chapter 2** | **Show Dialog** and a modal dialog will pop up:

Creating a modeless dialog

Now we will create a modeless dialog and see the difference between modal and modeless dialogs. Update the showDialog function as shown here:

```
function showDialog() {
  var html = HtmlService.createHtmlOutputFromFile('Index');
  DocumentApp.getUi()
  .showModelessDialog(html, 'Greeting');
}
```

Note that the showModalDialog method has been changed to showModelessDialog.

Modeless dialogs do not prevent you from doing other things, such as editing the document, and you can drag the dialog around as shown here:

Debugging your script

Logging the values of variables at a few points is essential when testing and debugging your code. The Logger class is a helpful tool to do this and has a few methods that are essential to debug your code.

Update the showDialog function as shown here:

```
function showDialog() {
  var ui = DocumentApp.getUi();

  var response = ui.prompt(
      'Greeting',
      'Will you enter your name below?',
      ui.ButtonSet.YES_NO
  );

  if (response.getSelectedButton() == ui.Button.YES) {
    Logger.log('Your name is %s.', response.getResponseText());
  } else if (response.getSelectedButton() == ui.Button.NO) {
```

```
      Logger.log('You clicked \'NO\' button');
   } else {
      Logger.log('You closed the dialog.');
   }
}
```

Run the `showDialog` function as usual from the **Add-ons** menu. Do anything, for example, enter your name and click on **Yes** or **No** or close the dialog.

Now within the script editor, press *Ctrl + Enter* (Windows) or Command + *Enter* (Mac) or from the **View** menu, select **Logs**, then you can see the logged text with a timestamp as shown here:

```
teAddonMenu()

                                                                    ×
   Logs

       [15-09-26 12:53:02:919 PDT] Your name is Ramalingam.
```

For a more detailed study of the `Logger` future, create the function `debug` as shown here:

```
function debug(){
   var square = 0;
   for(var i = 0; i < 10; i++){
      square = i * i;
      Logger.log(square);
   }
}
```

Run the debug function and see the Logger result as shown here:

```
Logs

[15-09-27 01:41:37:956 IST] 0.0
[15-09-27 01:41:37:956 IST] 1.0
[15-09-27 01:41:37:957 IST] 4.0
[15-09-27 01:41:37:958 IST] 9.0
[15-09-27 01:41:37:958 IST] 16.0
[15-09-27 01:41:37:959 IST] 25.0
[15-09-27 01:41:37:959 IST] 36.0
[15-09-27 01:41:37:960 IST] 49.0
[15-09-27 01:41:37:960 IST] 64.0
[15-09-27 01:41:37:961 IST] 81.0
```

In addition to logging, you can use the debug feature of the editor. In the editor, you set break points at one or more lines. To do so, click once on the line number on which you want to set a break point. A red dot will be toggled just on the left-hand side of the line number, as shown here:

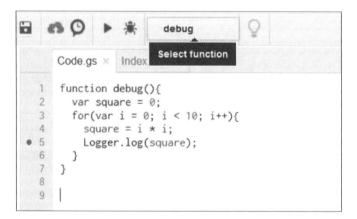

Select the debug function that you want to debug in the **Select function** selector if it is not already selected. Click on the **Debug** button (shown as an insect) to the left of the function selector. The function is executed up to the break point and then pauses. The edit window is split horizontally and shows the object and its values in the bottom part of the window as shown here:

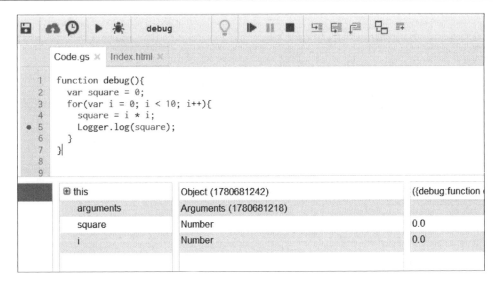

Click on the **Continue debugging** button to see the values on every cycle of the
`for` loop.

  You can experiment with the other features such as step into, step over,
and step out.

To exit the debugging session, click on the **Stop debugging** button and remember
to remove (toggle) all the break points.

Summary

In this chapter, you learned about many type of dialog and how to create and
display them, you found out how to use the `Logger` class to log values, and you
also saw how to debug your script. In the next chapter, you will learn about Gmail
and Contacts.

Downloading the example code

You can download the example code files for this book from your account at http://www.packtpub.com. If you purchased this book elsewhere, you can visit http://www.packtpub.com/support and register to have the files e-mailed directly to you.

You can download the code files by following these steps:

- Log in or register to our website using your e-mail address and password.
- Hover the mouse pointer on the **SUPPORT** tab at the top.
- Click on **Code Downloads & Errata**.
- Enter the name of the book in the **Search** box.
- Select the book for which you're looking to download the code files.
- Choose from the drop-down menu where you purchased this book from.
- Click on **Code Download**.

Once the file is downloaded, please make sure that you unzip or extract the folder using the latest version of:

- WinRAR / 7-Zip for Windows
- Zipeg / iZip / UnRarX for Mac
- 7-Zip / PeaZip for Linux

3
Parsing and Sending E-mails

In the previous chapter, you learned how to create basic GAS elements such as custom menu, dialog, and toast. You also learned how to debug your script codes. In this chapter, you will learn many real-world Gmail and Contacts applications including a mail merger application.

In this chapter, if you go through left and right square brackets inside code like [[value]], then replace value with the actual value including the brackets.

For example, if the e-mail ID is example@emample.com and you go through My email id [[emailid]] \n, then replace it with My email id example@example.com \n.

Creating Gmail Contacts by script

You can create Gmail Contacts by script using the createContact method of the ContactsApp class. For example, if the name is Anika Sumi and the e-mail ID is anika@example.com, then the ContactsApp.createContact("Anika", "Sumi", "anika@example.com") code will create the expected contact.

To know more available methods of the ContactsApp class, in the code editor, type ContactsApp and . (a dot) next to it. Then, you can view all the available methods with parameter details in code hint as shown in the following screenshot:

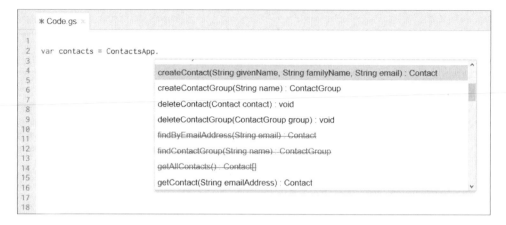

You can see deprecated methods struck out in the preceding screenshot; you are advised not to use those methods.

Accessing Sheet, cell, range, and offset

A Google Sheet's spreadsheet has one or more Sheets or tabs in it. Sheets are indexed from left to right starting from 0. For example, the left-most Sheet is referred to by the index 0, the next one by 1, and so on. In GAS, we can refer to a Sheet by its index or by its name.

For example:

- The getSheets() method returns an array of Sheet objects. From the array, we can refer to an individual Sheet by its index.

- The getSheetByName("Contacts") function returns a Sheet object with the name Contacts.

In Google Sheets, column label starts from the letter *A*, and is counted in a programmatic point of view, from left to right starting with the number 1. For example, column *A* is 1, *B* is 2, and so on. Rows are identified by their respective label numbers. In GAS, we can reference a cell or a range of cells by *A1* notation or by separate row and column numbers.

For example:

- The `getRange('D1:F10')` method returns a `Range` object referencing the cells from *D1* to *F10*

- The `getRange(1,4,10,3)` method returns a `Range` object referencing the same range *D1:F10*

Offset is an indirect referencing method to refer to a cell/range from a base cell reference. An offset reference is determined by how many rows and columns it shifted from the base cell.

For example, if the base cell is *D1*, then the `offset(10,3)` method returns the range *D1:F10*.

Reading and writing the Sheet data

Often you need to read and/or write data to/from the Sheet. Usually, use the `getValue` method to read a value from a cell and the `getValues` method to read values from a range. The `getValue` method returns a single value and the `getValues` method returns a 2-dimensional array of values. To write single value and 2-dimensional array of values, use `setValue` and `setValues` methods respectively.

Building a Gmail Contact search application

Now, we will create an application to search existing contacts. This application is able to search and list your Gmail Contacts in Sheets. Create a new Sheet and rename `Sheet1` to `Contacts` and set it up as shown in the following screenshot. Create a button and assign the function name `searchContacts` to it, as you learned in the previous chapter.

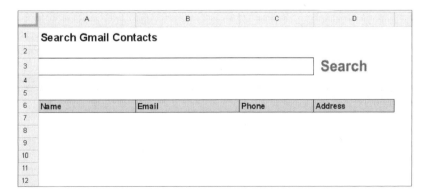

Create the `searchContacts` function as listed here:

```
function searchContacts(){

    var SheetContacts = SpreadsheetApp.getActiveSpreadsheet()
        .getSheetByName("Contacts");

    // Read input from cell A3
    var searchCriteria = SheetContacts.getRange("A3").getValue();

    //  First 10 contacts.
    //  [You can change this limit, but advised to keep small.]
    var numOfContacts = 10;

    // Clear existing sheet data
    SheetContacts.getRange(7,1,numOfContacts,4).clear();
```

Here, `clear` is the `Range` object's method to clear everything including format and formula, in a range of cells. You can use the `clear` method of the `Sheet` object to clear the entire Sheet. Alternatively, you can use the `clearContent` method to clear content only.

```
    // Returns an array of contacts where
    // contacts name matches with search text.
    var contacts = ContactsApp.getContactsByName(searchCriteria);

    //  Limit number of contacts.
    if(contacts.length > numOfContacts) contacts.length =
    numOfContacts;

    var cell = SheetContacts.getRange("A7");

    for(var i in contacts){
      var name = contacts[i].getFullName();
      var email = contacts[i].getEmails()[0];

      if(email) email = email.getAddress();
      else email = "";

      // For simplicity get the first phone number
      var phone = contacts[i].getPhones()[0];

      if (phone) phone = phone.getPhoneNumber();
      else phone = "";
```

```
        // For simplicity get the first address
        var address = contacts[i].getAddresses()[0];

        if(address) address = address.getAddress();
        else address = "";

        // cell.offset(rowOffset, columnOffset)
        cell.offset(i,0).setValue(name);
        cell.offset(i,1).setValue(email);
        cell.offset(i,2).setValue(phone);
        cell.offset(i,3).setValue(address);
    }
};
```

 Do not copy paste the preceding code, but edit it yourself. By doing so, you'll be aware of available method signatures (method names and parameters) of classes such as `SpreadsheetApp`, `ContactApp`, and `Contact` with the help of the script editor's code hint feature.

After you have edited and saved code without error, turn to the spreadsheet window. If you enter a search term in the *A3* cell (search box) and click on **Search**, then the first 10 contacts will be listed as shown in the following screenshot (the listed contacts details vary as per your Gmail username and contacts):

What if you want to update the listed contacts by the searchContacts function? For example, you may want to update the phone number and/or address of a contact. To update contact fields, we will create another function called updateContacts. Before creating that, in the Contacts Sheet, add a button next to **Search** named **Update** and assign function name updateContacts as shown in the following screenshot:

Update those field values you would like to update. Now create the function listed here:

```
function updateContacts(){
  var SheetContacts = SpreadsheetApp.getActiveSpreadsheet()
      .getSheetByName("Contacts");

  var cell = SheetContacts.getRange("A7");

  var numOfContacts = 10;

  for(var i = 0; i < numOfContacts; i++){

    var email = cell.offset(0, 1).getValue();

    // Skip if email field is null
    if(!email) continue;

    var contact = ContactsApp.getContact(email);

    // Skip if contact is null or undefined
    if(!contact) continue;

    var name = cell.offset(i, 0).getValue();
```

```
    // Skip if name field is null
    if(!name) continue;
    contact.setFullName(name);


    var phone = cell.offset(i, 2).getValue().toString();

    // Returns phone numbers as an array
    var contPhone =
    contact.getPhones(ContactsApp.Field.MAIN_PHONE)[0];

    // Update main phone number if exist otherwise add.
    if(phone){

      if(contPhone){
        contPhone.setPhoneNumber(phone);
      } else {
        contact.addPhone(ContactsApp.Field.MAIN_PHONE, phone);
      }

    }



    var address = cell.offset(i, 3).getValue().toString();

    // Returns address as an array
    var contAddress = contact
        .getAddresses(ContactsApp.Field.HOME_ADDRESS)[0];

    // Update home address if exist otherwise add.
    if(address){

      if(contAddress) {
        contAddress.setAddress(address);
      } else {
        contact.addAddress(ContactsApp.Field.HOME_ADDRESS,
        address);
      }

    }

  }
};
```

The preceding function retrieves contacts by the given e-mail ID; and, for each contact, it also retrieves field values and updates/adds those field values with the Sheet values. This function can update/add full name, phone, and address fields but not the e-mail ID.

Building the Gmail parser application

The `parseEmail` function is able to check 10 latest inbox threads, extract the **from** field and body text from unread messages, and put the gathered data in the left-most tab of the Sheet. Create the `parseEmail` function as listed here:

```
/**
 *  Gets content of latest unread message in Gmail inbox
 *     and puts gathered data in left most tab of Sheets.
 *
 */
function parseEmail(){

  // Left most sheet/tab
  var emailSheet = SpreadsheetApp.getActiveSpreadsheet()
      .getSheets()[0];

  // Clear the entire sheet.
  emailSheet.clear();

  // Checks maximum 10 threads
  var thread = GmailApp.getInboxThreads(0,10);

  var row = 1;

  for(var thrd in thread){
    var messages = thread[thrd].getMessages();

    for (var msg in messages) {
      var message = messages[msg];

      if(message && message.isUnread())
      emailSheet.getRange(row,1).setValue(message.getFrom());

      emailSheet.getRange(row++,2)
      .setValue(message.getPlainBody());
    }
  }

};
```

You can use `RegExp` to extract only the required data from the message body text.

Properties service

GAS provides the properties service to store and/or to retrieve project-related data. The data organized as key/value pairs, can be set manually or by script codes. The following screenshot shows how you can set properties manually. To see this dialog, click on the **File** menu and select **Project properties**:

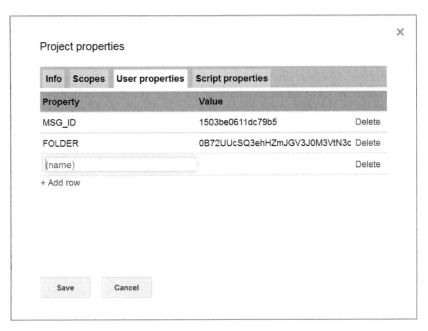

 You can use manually created project properties in script codes, but the properties created by code sometimes may not be visible in the **Project properties** dialog. You can create, update, or delete project properties in codes.

In the next task, we are going to use project properties.

Downloading Gmail attachments to Drive

The saveEmailAttachmentsToDrive function can download Gmail attachments to Drive. In this function PropertiesService is used to avoid repeated downloading of the same attachment. The createFolder_ function is used to create folders, if not already exist, with the given name in Drive.

If any function name is appended with _, then it will not be listed under the **Run** menu. You cannot run these functions directly, but they can be called from the other functions. These are called **private functions**.

You can create the `createFolder_` function in the same script file along with the `saveEmailAttachmentsToDrive` function or in a separate script file such as `Library.gs`:

```
/**
 *   Checks latest 100 inbox threads,
 *     saves attachments in 'Gmail attachments' folder,
 *
 */
function saveEmailAttachmentsToDrive(){

   // Create 'Gmail Attachments' folder if not exists.
   createFolder_('Gmail attachments');

   // Get inbox threads starting from the latest one to 100.
   var threads = GmailApp.getInboxThreads(0, 100);

   var messages = GmailApp.getMessagesForThreads(threads);

   var folderID = PropertiesService.getUserProperties()
       .getProperty("FOLDER");

   var file, folder = DriveApp.getFolderById(folderID);

   for (var i = 0 ; i < messages.length; i++) {
     for (var j = 0; j < messages[i].length; j++) {
       if(!messages[i][j].isUnread()){

         var msgId = messages[i][j].getId();

         // Assign '' if MSG_ID is undefined.
         var oldMsgId = PropertiesService.getUserProperties()
             .getProperty('MSG_ID') || '';

         if(msgId > oldMsgId){
           var attachments = messages[i][j].getAttachments();
```

```
        for (var k = 0; k < attachments.length; k++) {
          PropertiesService.getUserProperties()
            .setProperty('MSG_ID', messages[i][j].getId());

          try {
            file = folder.createFile(attachments[k]);
            Utilities.sleep(1000);// Wait before next iteration.
          } catch (e) {
            Logger.log(e);
          }
        }

      }
      else return;

    }
   }
  }

};
```

The preceding function calls the following createFolder_ function with the folder name as an argument. The function createFolder_ looks for the given folder, creates if it does not exist, and returns its unique ID:

```
function createFolder_(name) {
  var folder, folderID, found = false;

  /*
   * Returns collection of all user folders as an iterator.
   * That means it do not return all folder names at once,
   * but you should get them one by one.
   *
   */
  var folders = DriveApp.getFolders();

  while (folders.hasNext()) {
    folder = folders.next();
    if (folder.getName() == name) {
      folderID = folder.getId();
      found = true;
      break;
    }
  };
```

```
  if (!found) {
    folder = DriveApp.createFolder(name);
    folderID = folder.getId();
  };

  PropertiesService.getUserProperties()
    .setProperty("FOLDER", folderID);

  return folderID;
}
```

In the preceding function the `getFolders` method is an iterator method. An iterator does not return all the data in one go, but only the current data. To get successive data, you should call next method repeatedly until `hasNext` became `false`.

Sending e-mails using the MailApp service

The `sendEmail` function is able to send e-mails with prefixed messages. Remember to replace e-mail ID and message text. This service is mainly used to send e-mails with limited methods (only `sendEmail` and `getRemainingDailyQuota`), and it cannot access your Gmail account. You can use the `GmailApp` class for more methods:

```
function sendEmail(){
  var to = "[[reciever email id]]";
  var message = "[[message]]\n";

  MailApp.sendEmail(to, "Chapter 3", message);
}
```

Sending an e-mail notification on Form submission

Imagine if you created a Form and presented it to many users. It would be tedious to open the response Sheet every time to verify whether any user has submitted the Form or not. The problem would be worse if you created many Forms and sent them to many users. It will be helpful receiving a notification e-mail whenever there is a Form submission.

For this task, create a Form with three fields as shown in the following screenshot:

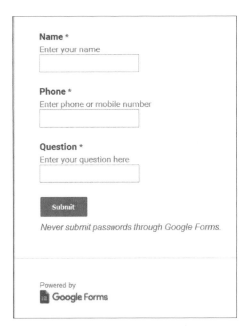

Submit the test data from a live form. Your submitted data will be saved in a response Sheet named something like `Form Responses 1`. The column headers will be as per your Form fields as shown in the following screenshot. Data may vary as per your input.

In the script file, you need to make the following changes:

1. Enter the `sendEmail` function mentioned from the following code.

2. Replace the receiver's e-mail ID. If you run this function, then it will send an e-mail with the last submitted data (bottom-most row) in the response Sheet.

3. Check the Sheet's actual name and the name used in the code; they should be exactly the same. If you are not sure, right-click on the Sheet name and select **Rename...**.

4. Copy the Sheet name from the **Rename** dialog and paste it in the
    following code:

```
function sendEmail(){
    var sheet = SpreadsheetApp.getActiveSpreadsheet()
        .getSheetByName("Form Responses 1");

    var lastRow = sheet.getLastRow();
    var lastCol = sheet.getLastColumn();
    var data = sheet.getRange(lastRow,1,1,lastCol)
        .getValues()[0];

    var to = "[[ receiver email id]]";
    var message = "Name: " + data[1] + "\n";

    message += "Phone: " + data[2] + "\n";
    message += "Question: " + data[3] + "\n";

    // MailApp.sendEmail(recipient, subject, body);
    MailApp.sendEmail(to, "Chapter 3", message);
}
```

You created a Form and a function to send response data to an e-mail ID. Creating
a trigger so as to run the `sendEmail` function as soon as a Form is submitted will
complete this task.

Creating triggers manually

To create a trigger, in the code editor click on **Resources** and select **Current project's
triggers** then the **Current project's triggers** dialog will open. Already created triggers
will be listed in this dialog, otherwise a link to create a new trigger will appear. Click
on the **No triggers set up. Click here to add one now** link. Select the options from
the dropdowns as shown in the following screenshot:

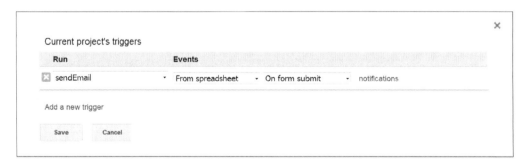

Under the **Run** heading, select the `sendEmail` function for which you want to create the trigger. Select **From spreadsheet** and **On form submit** under the **Events** heading as shown in the preceding screenshot.

If a Form user submits data to the spreadsheet, the trigger will run the `sendEmail` function.

For more info on triggers, please go to `https://developers.google.com/apps-script/guides/triggers/`.

Creating and deleting triggers by script

You can create or delete triggers programmatically as shown in the following sample code:

```
/**
 * Deletes all the triggers.
 *
 */
function deleteTriggers(){
  var triggers = ScriptApp.getProjectTriggers();

  triggers.forEach(function(trigger){

    try{
      ScriptApp.deleteTrigger(trigger);
    } catch(e) {
      throw e.message;
    };

    Utilities.sleep(1000);

  });

};

function createTrigger(){
  var ss = SpreadsheetApp.getActiveSpreadsheet();

  // Create new trigger
  ScriptApp.newTrigger("sendEmail")
    .forSpreadsheet(ss).onFormSubmit().create();
};
```

In the deleteTriggers function, the Utilities service's sleep method is used to pause the script temporarily for the specified milliseconds. Otherwise, you may experience the Too many service invocation... error.

Forwarding e-mails if the specific keyword is found in the message body

The forwardEmails function is able to forward e-mail messages, if a specific keyword is found in the body text to a prefixed e-mail ID. Be cautious about the number of iterations of the for loop while testing your code so that you can avoid lot of messages forwarded in error:

```
/**
 *   1. Checks all unread inbox threads and messages.
 *
 *   2. If specific keyword found then forwards it to another
 *      recipient.
 *
 *   3. Marks that message as Read.
 *
 */
function forwardEmails() {
  var recipient = "[[forward email id]]";
  /*
   *   Use keywords separated by '|'.
   *   For example: "purchase | invoice"
   *
   */
  var words = "keywords list";
  var regExp = new RegExp(words,'g');

  var len = GmailApp.getInboxUnreadCount();

  for (var i = 0; i < len; i++) {
    // get 'i'th thread in inbox
    var thread = GmailApp.getInboxThreads(i,1)[0];

    // get all messages in 'i'th thread
    var messages = thread.getMessages();
```

```
    var msgLen = messages.length;
    var isAllMarkedRead = true;

    // iterate over each message
    // CAUTION: limit loop iterations for initial testing.
    for (var j = 0; j < 5 /* msgLen */; j++) {
      var message = messages[j];

      if(message.isUnread()){
        var bodyText = message.getPlainBody();
        var test = regExp.exec(bodyText);
        message.forward(recipient);
        isAllMarkedRead = false;
        message.markRead();
      }

    };

    if(isAllMarkedRead) len++;
    Utilities.sleep(1000);
  }

};
```

Sending e-mail with attachments

You can attach any type of file to your e-mail message by setting options as shown in the following code. The following code attaches the active spreadsheet's left-most Sheet content as PDF.

```
function sendEmailWithAttachments(){
  var file = SpreadsheetApp.getActiveSpreadsheet()
      .getAs(MimeType.PDF);

  // MailApp.sendEmail(recipient, subject, body, options)
  MailApp.sendEmail(
    "[[ Recipient email id ]]",
    "Chapter 3",
    "",
    {
      attachments: [file],
      name: 'Chapter 3 test attachment'
    }
  );

}
```

Embedding inline images in an e-mail message

To embed images such as a logo in your e-mail message, you may use HTML code instead of plain text. Upload your image to Google Drive, retrieve, and use that file ID in code:

```
function sendEmail(){
  var sheet = SpreadsheetApp.getActiveSpreadsheet()
      .getSheetByName("Form Responses 1");

  var lastRow = sheet.getLastRow();
  var lastCol = sheet.getLastColumn();
  var data = sheet.getRange(lastRow,1,1,lastCol).getValues()[0];

  var image = DriveApp.getFileById("[[image file's id in Drive
  ]]").getBlob();

  var to = "[[Recipient email id ]]";
  var message = '<img src="cid:logo" />';

  message += "<p>Name: " + data[1] + "</p>";
  message += "<p>Phone: " + data[2] + "</p>";
  message += "<p>Question: " + data[3] + "</p>";

  MailApp.sendEmail(
    to,
    "Chapter 3 inline image example",
    "",
    {
      inlineImages:{ logo:image },
      htmlBody:message
    }
  );
}
```

Building an e-mail merger application

Sending personalized e-mails to hundreds of recipients at a time might be a time consuming task. Composing the draft and entering the subject and recipient's e-mail ID for each message might be tedious too. Using this mail merger application, you can send the same kind of information to all recipients, but customized to some extent. For example, greeting an individual.

The first step is creating a draft in your Gmail as shown in the following screenshot. The draft is used as a template. You can use any special character to enclose the text to be replaced. In the draft, the code shown in the following screenshot uses left (<<) and right (>>) angled brackets to replace the first name with the **First Name** column data in an `EmailList` Sheet. You can include any other placeholder or field as per your requirement. Set up the draft, but don't send it now:

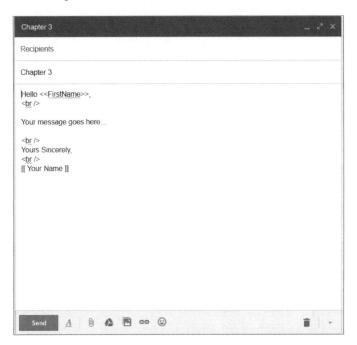

Create a Sheet with the name as `EmailList` in a new Sheet or existing Sheet. Create the column headers as shown here:

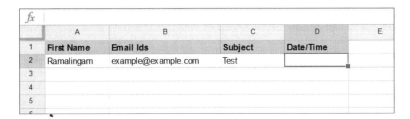

Create functions as shown in the following code, in the script editor. Replace the draft and sender name with actual values. Set `maxEmails` (this code uses 50) by considering your daily e-mail sending quota:

```
// Returns your draft text.
function getDraftBody(draftName){
  var drafts = GmailApp.getDraftMessages();

  for(var i in drafts)
    if( drafts[i].getSubject() == draftName )
      return drafts[i].getPlainBody();
}


function sendEmails(){
  // EmailList sheet column numbers, 0 based.
  const FIRST_NAME_COL = 0;
  const EMAIL_IDS_COL = 1;
  const SUB_COL = 2;
  const DATE_COL = 3;

  var maxEmails = 50;
  var draftName = "Chapter 3";// Draft's subject name

  var draftBody = getDraftBody(draftName);
  var quotaLeft = MailApp.getRemainingDailyQuota();

  var ss = SpreadsheetApp.getActive();
  var sheet = ss.getSheetByName("EmailList");

  // Gets all sheet data as a 2-dimensional array.
  var data = sheet.getDataRange().getValues();
  var header = data.shift();

  for(var i=0,count=0; count < maxEmails && count < quotaLeft
      && i < data.length; ++i){
    var firstName = data[i][FIRST_NAME_COL];
    var recipient = data[i][EMAIL_IDS_COL];
    var subject = data[i][SUB_COL];
    var htmlBody = draftBody.replace("<<FirstName>>", firstName);

    if(recipient){
      GmailApp.sendEmail(
        recipient,
```

```
            subject,
            "",
            {
              name:"[[ Sender Name ]]",
              htmlBody:htmlBody
            }
          );

        data[i][DATE_COL] = new Date();

        ++count;
      }
    };

    // Inserts header at top of the array.
    data.unshift(header);

    // Stores values of array in sheet.
    sheet.getRange(1, 1, data.length, header.length)
      .setValues(data);
  }
```

Populate data in the EmailList Sheet. To send e-mails, run the sendEmails function. The <<FirstName>> field in your draft will be replaced as per your **First Name** column data in the EmailList Sheet. That's it!

Congratulations! You have created a working e-mail merger application.

Summary

In this chapter, you learned about ContactsApp, MailApp, and GmailApp classes and their methods. Using these classes, you created many useful real-world applications including an e-mail merger application. In the next chapter, you will learn how to create Forms programmatically using FormApp and HtmlService classes. Also you will learn about doGet and doPost simple trigger functions.

4

Creating Interactive Forms

In the previous chapter, you learned about many of the features of `GmailApp` and `ContactApp` and you built lots of real-world applications. In this chapter, you will learn how to create Forms programmatically using `FormApp` and `HtmlService`. Also, you will learn about the `doGet` and `doPost` functions.

Creating Forms using script

In *Chapter 1, Introducing Google Apps Scripts*, you created a Form manually, but this time we will create Forms programmatically by script. First of all, we will create a Form with four choices and an **Other** option choice. For simplicity, we add places as a multiple choice radio group. Each choice is exclusively selectable. Create the function `createForm` as shown here in a spreadsheet code file:

```
function createForm() {

  var places = ["Place 1","Place 2","Place 3","Place 4"];

  var form = FormApp.create("Vacation Form");

  form.addMultipleChoiceItem()
    .setTitle('Where will you go for vacation?')
    .setChoiceValues(places)
    .showOtherOption(true);

}
```

The `places` variable holds a few random places, and you can assign any place name and any number of places as an array of strings. The `create` method of `FormApp` class creates a form titled `Vacation Form` in your Drive's root folder (`My Drive`). On running the function, the created Form will look like this:

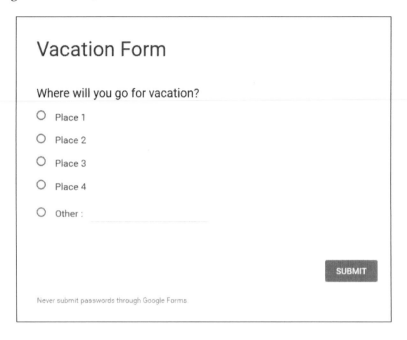

The choices are hardcoded in the code. If you would like to change any choice or add more choices, then you should edit the code to make the required changes. If you need to change the choices frequently, it might become irritating or hard to edit the code every time. Now we will add place names from spreadsheet's data rather than them being hardcoded. Add or rename an existing sheet as `Places` and add a few place names in it as shown here:

Now update the `createForm` function as shown here:

```
function createForm() {

  var ThisSpreadsheet = SpreadsheetApp.getActive();
  var SheetPlaces = ThisSpreadsheet.getSheetByName("Places");

  // Load 'Places' sheet data as a 2-dimensional array.
  var data = SheetPlaces.getDataRange().getValues();

  // remove the header row
  data.shift();

  var places = [];

  // Populate the places array with the first column's data
  data.forEach(function(row){
    places.push(row[0]);
  });

  // Create a new form
  var form = FormApp.create("Vacation Form");

  form.addMultipleChoiceItem()
    .setTitle('Where will you go for a vacation?')
    .setChoiceValues(places)
    .showOtherOption(true);

}
```

The preceding function will create a Form with the choices' text retrieved from the Sheet's data. The choices' text and/or number of choices can be varied as per your Sheet's data. If you would like to make any changes in the choices' text, then it is enough to edit the Sheet's data, and you do not need to edit the code.

When you run the function just mentioned, it will create a Form named Vacation Form in the My Drive folder. To open the Form in edit mode, double-click or right-click (context click) on Form name and go to **Open with | Google Forms**. The following screenshot shows what the Form would look like in edit mode. You can make any adjustments and/or perform formatting in edit mode:

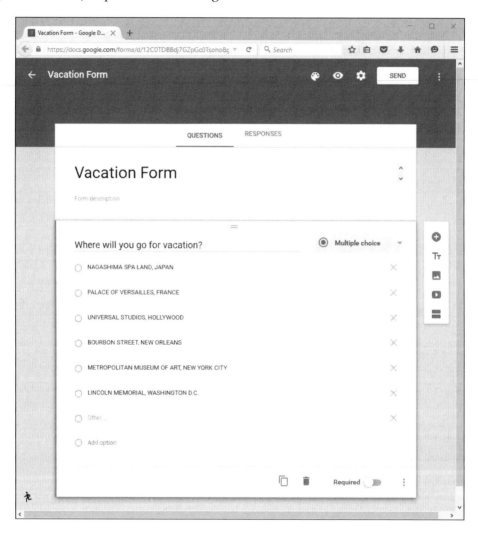

To open the live Form, right-click (context click) on the Form name, click on **Get link**, copy the link, and then paste the link in your browser's address bar. The following screenshot shows what the live Form will look like:

You can share the live Form link with your users. Your user's responses are stored in the Form itself. You can see responses in the Form editor, or link a spreadsheet to it to view the responses, as shown:

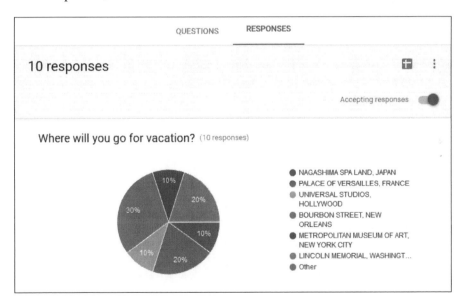

You can link Form responses to a spreadsheet manually by clicking on the icon in the top right-hand corner of the Form editor. A new `Form Responses` Sheet will be created in the selected spreadsheet.

To programmatically link a spreadsheet, use the following code:

```
form.setDestination( FormApp.DestinationType.SPREADSHEET,
ThisSpreadsheet.getId() ); // Replace with your spreadsheet's ID
```

Publishing the script as a web application

You can create awesome web pages/applications by publishing your script as a web application. In this section, you'll see how to publish a script. Start by creating a new Sheet and entering the following code in the script editor:

```
function doGet(){
   var str = "Hello world!";
   return ContentService.createTextOutput(str);
}
```

The `doGet` function will be executed whenever a HTTP/HTTPS request is sent to the script. In the preceding code, `ContentService` is used to return a string to the browser. Content service can be used to return any type of content including simple text, HTML, XML, JSON, CSV, and so on.

To publish the script, within the script editor, navigate to **Publish | Deploy as web app…**. A new **Deploy as web app** dialog will open as shown here:

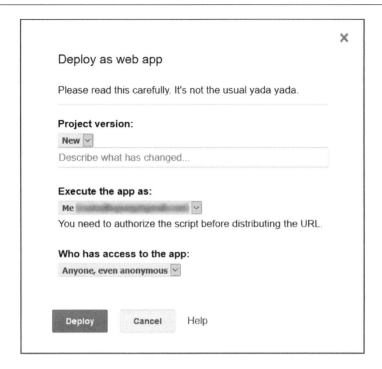

Select any one of the existing project versions or select **New** to create a new project version. There will be two choices under the **Execute the app as** option, **Me** and **User**, accessing the web app. For this application, select **Me** (your user ID). This means the script will run on behalf of your user ID. If you had selected the second option then the script would run on behalf of the user who is accessing the application. Select **Anyone, even anonymous** under the **Who has access to the app** option.

> There are two more choices **Only myself** and **Anyone** available under the **Who has access to the app** option. Select **Only myself** if you would only like to get access to the published app. Select **Anyone** if you would like to give access to others, but please be aware that the others should be logged in with their Google user ID. If you select **Anyone, even anonymous**, then your user can be anyone and does not need to be logged in. They do not even need to be a Google user.

Finally, click on the **Deploy** button. Then another dialog will open as shown in the following screenshot:

 If you are publishing the script for the first time, then you need to authorize the script. Authorization is initiated before web app deployment. Click **Allow** in the authorization dialog.

In this dialog, you can see the published URL under the **Current web app URL** textbox. You can copy and paste this URL in a new browser window/tab address bar to see the working of your web application. For the preceding code, the text returned will be **Hello world!** Click **OK** to close the dialog.

 If you make any changes in your code, then you should publish the new version again, otherwise the updates will not take effect. Alternatively, you can use the **latest code** URL for development purposes.

HtmlService

At the beginning of this chapter, you created a Form using script codes. However, this Form is a static one, meaning you cannot add dynamic formatting or script on the client side. You can perform formatting and calculations, if there are any to be done, on the server side only.

HtmlService allows scripts to return HTML or web pages to clients. For security reasons the HTML content, including CSS and JavaScript, are compiled and sandboxed by Caja compiler before returning to the client browser. The returned web page(s) can interact with server-side GAS functions using the google.script.run API methods.

The advantages of using `HtmlService` are:

- You can use CSS and client-side JavaScript
- You can create dynamic HTML forms rather than static Forms
- You can work on client-side HTML and server-side script codes separately

`HtmlService` can create HTML codes from templates. The **templates** are HTML files mixed with HTML markup and scripts (these are called **scriptlets** and are executed on the server side).

Scriptlets enclosed by `<?` and `?>` execute but output nothing to the enclosing HTML. In other words, they do not alter the surrounding HTML code. Scriptlets enclosed by `<?=` and `?>` return the output to the surrounding HTML code. Any functions inside scriptlets can call functions of other scriptlets or server-script functions, but server functions cannot call functions within scriptlets.

For further reading on scriptlet tags, visit: `https://developers.google.com/apps-script/guides/html/templates`.

Creating a Form using HtmlService

Create a `Form.html` file, which we are going to use as an HTML template and enter the following code in it:

```html
<!-- Form.html -->
<!DOCTYPE html>
<html>

  <head>
    <base target="_top">
  </head>

  <body>
    <form>
      <h4>Where will you go for vacation?</h4>

      <input type="radio" name="places" value="Place 1" />Place 1

      <br />
      <input type="radio" name="places" value="Place 2" />Place 2

      <br />
```

```
        <input type="radio" name="places" value="Place 3" />Place 3

        <br />
        <input type="radio" name="places" value="Place 4" />Place 4

        <br />
        <br />
        <input type="submit" value="SUBMIT" />
    </form>
  </body>
</html>
```

Use the same name attribute value for radio type input fields so that they are all grouped together. This means they will work exclusively. Update the doGet function in the Code.gs file to render the previously mentioned HTML form, as follows:

```
// Code.gs
function doGet() {
  var template = HtmlService.createTemplateFromFile("Form.html");
  var html = template.evaluate();

  return HtmlService.createHtmlOutput(html);
}
```

Publish the script and enter the published URL in your browser's address bar. The basic HTML form returned is shown here:

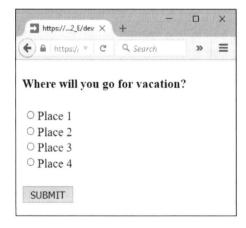

To populate places automatically from spreadsheet data, update the HTML code as shown here:

```
<form>
    <h4>Where will you go for vacation?</h4>
    <? for (var i in places) { ?>
      <input type="radio" name="places"
      value="<?= places[i] ?>" /><?= places[i] ?><br />
    <? } ?>
    <br />
    <input type="submit" value="SUBMIT" />
</form>
```

The scriptlet `<?= places[i] ?>` returns the *i*th element from the `places` array. You also need to update the `doGet` function as shown here:

```
function doGet() {
  // Replace with your spreadsheet's ID.
  var ss = SpreadsheetApp.openById("spreadsheet's id");
  var SheetPlaces = ss.getSheetByName("Places");

  var data = SheetPlaces.getDataRange().getValues();

  // Remove header row.
  data.shift();

  var places = [];

  // Populate the places array with the first column's data.
  data.forEach(function(row){
    places.push(row[0]);
  });

  var template = HtmlService.createTemplateFromFile("Form.html");

  // Assign the places array to the template object.
  template.places = places;

  var html = template.evaluate();
  return HtmlService.createHtmlOutput(html);
}
```

The `places` array is assigned to the template in the `doGet` function and referenced in the HTML template. Then, the output becomes the following:

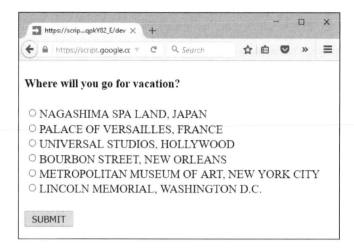

To submit this Form data to the spreadsheet, you need to add method and action attributes to the Form element:

```
<form method="post" action="<?= pubUrl ?>" >
```

Assign the published URL to the `template` object in the `doGet` function, for example:

```
template.pubUrl =
"https://script.google.com/macros/s/AKfycbzMqmOaaD-
TTDbycMl2AxF7dtn9EqxqZTwozcQBNHxe9hg4Kbc/exec";
```

You could also assign it as follows:

```
template.pubUrl = ScriptApp.getService().getUrl();
```

To process the submitted Form data, add a `doPost` function. The `doGet` or `doPost` functions execute as per the HTTP/HTTPS request method (GET and POST):

```
function doPost(e){
  // Replace with your spreadsheet's ID.
  var ss = SpreadsheetApp.openById("spreadsheet's id");

  var SheetResponses = ss.getSheetByName("Responses");

  // Create a 'Responses' sheet if it does not exist.
  if(!SheetResponses){
      SheetResponses = ss.insertSheet("Responses");
```

```
    };

    SheetResponses.appendRow([e.parameter.places]);

    return ContentService.createTextOutput(
        "Your response submitted successfully. Thank you!"
    );

}
```

After the Form is submitted, a thank you message is returned as the normal text content:

Submitting form using Google script API method

To submit data using the `google.script.run` API methods, add `onclick` property to the **Submit** button:

```
<input type="submit" value="SUBMIT"
onclick="google.script.run.postFormDataToSheet(this.parentNode);"
/>
<!-- this.parentNode is the 'form' element -->
```

Create the `postFormDataToSheet` function as shown here:

```
function postFormDataToSheet(e){
    // Replace with your spreadsheet's ID.
    var ss = SpreadsheetApp.openById("spreadsheet's id");

    var SheetResponses = ss.getSheetByName("Responses");

    // Create a 'Responses' sheet if it does not exist.
    if(!SheetResponses){
        SheetResponses = ss.insertSheet("Responses");
    }

    SheetResponses.appendRow([e.places]);
}
```

To show Form submission result or error message, insert the `postData` function in a separate `<script>` tag and add success and failure handlers with a callback function as shown here:

```
<script>
  function postData(form) {
    google.script.run
      .withSuccessHandler(callback)
      .withFailureHandler(callback)
      .postFormDataToSheet(form);
  }

  function callback(msg) {
    alert(msg);
  }
</script>
```

Insert a return statement with a message to the user at the end of the `postFormDataToSheet` function.

To add the `User` object to the `google.script.run` API calls, add the `withUserObject` method along with the success and failure handlers:

The complete HTML code with the `user` object is shown here:

```
<!DOCTYPE html>
<html>
  <head>
    <base target="_top">

    <script>
      function postData(form) {
        google.script.run
          .withSuccessHandler(showSuccess)
          .withFailureHandler(showError)
          .withUserObject(form)
          .postFormDataToSheet(form);
      }

      /*
       * msg -  the error or success message returned
       *        from the server.
       *
       * elem - the reference to the user object (form).
       *
```

```
    */
    function showSuccess(msg,elem) {
      var newElement = document.createElement("div");
      newElement.innerHTML = '<font color="green">'
        + msg + '</font>';
      elem.appendChild(newElement);
    }

    /*
     * msg -   the error or success message returned
     *         from the server.
     *
     * elem - the reference to the user object (form).
     *
     */
    function showError(msg,elem){
      var newElement = document.createElement("div");

      newElement.innerHTML = '<font color="red">'
        + msg + '</font>';

      elem.appendChild(newElement);
    }

  </script>
</head>

<body>
  <form>
    <h4>Where will you go for vacation?</h4>

    <? for (var i in places) { ?>
      <input type="radio" name="places"
        value="<?= places[i] ?>" /><?= places[i] ?>
      <br />
    <? } ?>

    <br />
    <input type="button" value="SUBMIT"
      onclick="postData(this.parentNode);" />
  </form>
</body>
</html>
```

The complete version of the `postFormDataToSheet` function is listed here:

```
function postFormDataToSheet(e){
  // Replace with your spreadsheet's ID.
  var ss = SpreadsheetApp.openById("spreadsheet's id");
  var SheetResponses = ss.getSheetByName("Responses");

  // Create 'Responses' sheet if it does not exist.
  if(!SheetResponses){
    SheetResponses = ss.insertSheet("Responses");
  }

  SheetResponses.appendRow([e.places]);

  return "Your response submitted successfully. Thank you!";
}
```

In this script, you used HTML code in a separate file, namely `Form.html`. This file is used as a template in the GAS server, and only the resulted markup and script code are returned to the user's browser. From the browser (the client side), we use the Google client-side JavaScript API (`google.script.run`) to interact with the GAS server. This is an AJAX-like interaction between the client and server. Here, the client and server are your browser and GAS server respectively.

Referencing HTML tags/elements (DOM elements) using plain JavaScript most of the time is a tedious task. To make life easier, you can use jQuery libraries. Also, you need not define CSS styles in the `<style>` tag yourself; rather you can use any officially-supported (by Google) third-party style sheets.

Creating forms using add-ons CSS and jQuery libraries

The same HTML code using the Google add-on CSS and jQuery libraries is as follows:

```
<!DOCTYPE html>
<html>
  <head>
    <base target="_top">

    <!-- Google's Add-ons stylesheet //-->
    <link rel="stylesheet"
      href="https://ssl.gstatic.com/docs/
      script/css/add-ons1.css" />
```

```
<script
 src="//ajax.googleapis.com/ajax/libs/
 jquery/1.10.2/jquery.min.js"></script>

<script>
  // on document load, assign postData function to submit
  // button's onclick property.
  $(function(){
    $("#btnSubmit").click(postData);
  });

  // Calls server side function 'postFormDataToSheet'
  // with form as the argument.
  function postData(){
    google.script.run
      .withSuccessHandler(showSuccess)
      .withFailureHandler(showError)
      .withUserObject(this)
      .postFormDataToSheet(this.parentNode);
  }

  /*
   * msg -  the error or success message returned
   *        from the server.
   *
   * elem - the reference to the user object (form).
   *
   */
  function showSuccess(msg,elem) {
    var div = $('<div id="error">
    <font color="green">' + msg + '</font></div>');
    $(elem).after(div);
  }

  /*
   * msg -  the error or success message returned
   *        from the server.
   *
   * elem - the reference to the user object (form).
   *
   */
  function showError(msg,elem) {
    var div = $('<div id="error"
    class="error">' + msg + '</div>');
    $(elem).after(div);
  }
</script>
</head>

<body>
```

```
<form>
  <h4>Where will you go for vacation?</h4>

  <? for (var i in places) { ?>
    <input type="radio" name="places"
      value="<?= places[i] ?>" /><?= places[i] ?>
    <br />
  <? } ?>

  <br />
  <input class="submit" id="btnSubmit"
    type="button" value="SUBMIT" />
</form>
</body>
</html>
```

Creating an e-voting application

The previous application appends each response to the Responses Sheet. But, we need to update the count against each choice. If we can make the selected choices increment by a counter then we can use the same application for e-voting purposes.

Edit the labels/headers for column *A* and *B* in the Places sheet as follows:

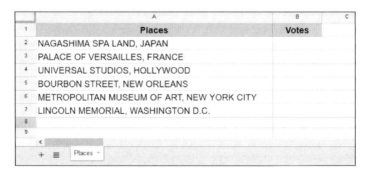

Update the HTML code in the Form.html file as shown here:

```
<!DOCTYPE html>
<html>
  <head>
    <base target="_top">

    <link rel="stylesheet"
      href="https://ssl.gstatic.com/docs/
      script/css/add-ons1.css" />
```

```
<script
 src="//ajax.googleapis.com/ajax/libs
 /jquery/1.10.2/jquery.min.js"></script>

<script>
  $(function(){
    $("#btnSubmit").click(postData);
  });

  function postData(){
    // Remove previous messages if any
    $("#error,#success").remove();

    // Disable the submit button until server returns
    // anything.
    this.disabled = true;

    // Call server function
    google.script.run
      .withSuccessHandler(showSuccess)
      .withFailureHandler(showError)
      .withUserObject(this)
      .postFormDataToSheet(this.parentNode);
  }

  /*
   * msg -  the error or success message returned
   *        from the server.
   *
   * elem - the reference to the user object (form).
   *
   */
  function showSuccess(msg,elem) {
    elem.disabled = false;
    var div = $('<div id="success">
    <font color="green">' + msg + '</font></div>');
    $(elem).after(div);
  }

  /*
   * msg -  the error or success message returned
   *        from the server.
   *
   * elem - the reference to the user object (form).
   *
```

```
      */
    function showError(msg,elem) {
      elem.disabled = false;
      var div = $('<div id="error" class="error">'
       + msg + '</div>');
      $(elem).after(div);
    }
  </script>
</head>

<body>
  <form>
    <h4>Where will you go for vacation?</h4>

    <? for (var i in places) { ?>
      <input type="radio" name="places"
       value="<?= i ?>" /><?= places[i] ?><br />
    <? } ?>

    <br />
    <input class="blue" id="btnSubmit" type="button"
     value="SUBMIT" />
  </form>
</body>
</html>
```

For this application keep the Form.html code as it is, but update the doGet and postFormDataToSheet functions as shown here:

```
function doGet() {
  // Replace with your spreadsheet's ID.
  var ss = SpreadsheetApp.openById("spreadsheet's id");
  var SheetPlaces = ss.getSheetByName("Places");

  var data = SheetPlaces.getDataRange().getValues();
  data.shift();

  var places = [];
  data.forEach(function(row){
    places.push(row[0]);
  });

  var template = HtmlService.createTemplateFromFile("Form.html");
```

```
    template.places = places;

    var html = template.evaluate();
    html.setTitle("eVoting");

    return HtmlService.createHtmlOutput(html);
}


function postFormDataToSheet(e){
    // Replace with your spreadsheet's ID.
    var ss = SpreadsheetApp.openById("spreadsheet's id");
    var SheetPlaces = ss.getSheetByName("Places");

    var data = SheetPlaces.getDataRange().getValues();

    var i = Number(e.places)+1;
    data[i][1]++;

    SheetPlaces.getRange(1, 1, data.length,
    data[0].length).setValues(data);

    return "Your response submitted successfully. Thank you!";
}
```

In this application, the responses are not appended, but the counts are incremented on every submission. A sample output is shown here:

	A	B	C
1	**Places**	**Votes**	
2	NAGASHIMA SPA LAND, JAPAN	7	
3	PALACE OF VERSAILLES, FRANCE	4	
4	UNIVERSAL STUDIOS, HOLLYWOOD	1	
5	BOURBON STREET, NEW ORLEANS	1	
6	METROPOLITAN MUSEUM OF ART, NEW YORK CITY	3	
7	LINCOLN MEMORIAL, WASHINGTON D.C.	9	
8			
9			

+ ≡   Places ▾

Creating a ticket reservation application

This application serves as an HTML form to the user to let them submit values to the server. This could be to reserve a ticket for a show, book a seat in a venue, book a room in a hotel, and many more purposes.

Create a spreadsheet and create column labels as shown in the following screenshot:

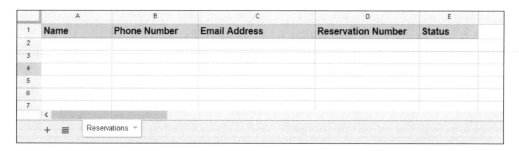

In the code file, create the doGet, doPost and cancelReservation functions:

```
function doGet(e) {
  // Maximum available
  const MAX_TICKETS = 25;

  // 'cancel' is a query string appended with the published URL.
  var cancel = e.parameter.cancel;

  if(cancel){
    var msg = cancelReservation(cancel);
    return ContentService.createTextOutput(msg);
  }

  // Replace with your spreadsheet's ID.
  var ss = SpreadsheetApp.openById("spreadsheet's id");
  var SheetReservations = ss.getSheetByName("Reservations");

  var data = SheetReservations.getDataRange().getValues();
  data.shift();

  var template = HtmlService.createTemplateFromFile("Form.html");
  template.available = MAX_TICKETS - data.length;

  if(template.available < 1)
  return ContentService.createTextOutput
  ("All tickets reserved, sorry!");

  // Use the following line of code for testing purposes only
```

```
// Replace with your development URL.
template.pubUrl =
"https://script.google.com/macros/s/ "
+ " AKfycbzIkrLEaMMRRYwOA_d_Tiy1TFtxUylaotB07HB4wZGW/dev";

// Uncomment the following line for the production use.
//template.pubUrl = ScriptApp.getService().getUrl();

var html = template.evaluate();
return HtmlService.createHtmlOutput(html);

}
```

In the preceding code, the doGet function initially checks for any query such as
cancel, appended with the URL. If cancel is present, then the cancelReservation
function is called, otherwise the HTML form is returned:

```
/**
 *   This function post the form data to the
 *   spreadsheet.
 *
 */
function doPost(e){
   // Replace with your spreadsheet's ID.
   var ss = SpreadsheetApp.openById("spreadsheet's id");
   var SheetReservations = ss.getSheetByName("Reservations");

   // name, phone_number and e-mail are form elements.
   var name = e.parameter.name;
   var phoneNumber = e.parameter.phone_number;
   var email = e.parameter.email;
   var ticketNumber = +new Date(); // current date as epoch number

   SheetReservations.appendRow(
      [name, phoneNumber, email, ticketNumber, "Reserved"]
   );

   // Use the following line of code for testing purposes only.
   // Replace with your development URl.
   var pubUrl =
   "https://script.google.com/macros/s/ "
   + " AKfycbzIkrLEaMMRRYwOA_d_Tiy1TFtxUylaotB07HB4wZGW/dev";

   // Uncomment the following line for production use.
```

```
   //pubUrl = ScriptApp.getService().getUrl();

   var emailBody = '<p>Thank you for registering. Your ticket
   number: ' + ticketNumber + '</p>';

   emailBody += '<p>You can <a href="'+ pubUrl +'?cancel=' +
   ticketNumber + '">click here</a> to cancel reservation.</p>';

   // Send confirmation e-mail with cancel link
   MailApp.sendEmail({
     to: email,
     subject: "Reservation Confirmation",
     htmlBody: emailBody
   });

   // Return confirmation text message to the browser.
   return ContentService.createTextOutput("Your ticket
   reserved and confirmation email has been sent.\nThank you!");
}


function cancelReservation(timestamp){

   // Replace with your spreadsheet id.
   var ss = SpreadsheetApp.openById("spreadsheet's id");

   var SheetReservations = ss.getSheetByName("Reservations");

   var data = SheetReservations.getDataRange().getValues();

   /*
    * Identify sheet row by timestamp if it matches
    * then mark as cancelled.
    *
    */
   for(var i = 0; i < data.length; i++){
     if(data[i][3] == timestamp) data[i][4] = "Cancelled";
   }

   // Replace the updated data in sheet
   SheetReservations.getRange(1, 1, data.length,
   data[0].length).setValues(data);

   return "Your reservation cancelled.";
}
```

The preceding function compares the ticket number (`timestamp`) with the existing data and, if that ticket number is present, then it is marked as cancelled.

Insert the following code in the `Form.html` file:

```
<!DOCTYPE html>
<html>
  <head>
    <base target="_top">
    <link rel="stylesheet"
     href="https://ssl.gstatic.com/docs/script/
     css/add-ons1.css" />
    <script
    src="//ajax.googleapis.com/ajax/libs/
    jquery/1.10.2/jquery.min.js"></script>
  </head>

  <body>
    <form method="post" action="<?= pubUrl ?>" >

        <h4>Reservation Form</h4>
        <p>Available: <?= available ?></p>

        <input type="text" name="name"
         placeholder="Enter your name"/>

        <br />
        <input type="text" name="phone_number"
         placeholder="Enter phone number"/>

        <br />
        <input type="text" name="email"
         placeholder="Enter email id"/>

        <br /><br />
        <input class="blue" id="btnSubmit"
         type="submit" value="Reserve"/>

    </form>
  </body>
</html>
```

A sample e-mail's body text is shown in the following screenshot:

Thank you for registering. Your ticket number: 1450299843245

You can click here to cancel reservation.

A sample output of the `Reservations` sheet is shown here:

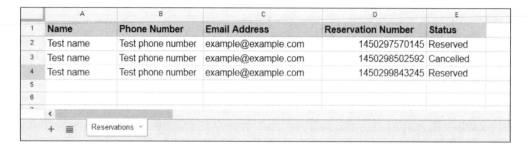

	A	B	C	D	E
1	Name	Phone Number	Email Address	Reservation Number	Status
2	Test name	Test phone number	example@example.com	1450297570145	Reserved
3	Test name	Test phone number	example@example.com	1450298502592	Cancelled
4	Test name	Test phone number	example@example.com	1450299843245	Reserved
5					
6					

Reservations

Summary

In this chapter, you learned how to create many useful real-life applications including a reservation system application. The next chapter will be focused on Google Calendar. You will learn how to create Calendar events and how to enable Google's advanced services. You will also learn to create Drive file routing and search applications.

5
Creating Google Calendar and Drive Applications

In the previous chapter, you learned how to create Forms programmatically using FormApp, ContentService, and HtmlService. Also, you learned how to use the doGet and doPost functions.

In this chapter, you will learn to:

- Create Calendar events
- Enable Google's advanced services
- Create a few Drive applications

The CalendarApp class

The CalendarApp class provides direct access to Calendar's basic service. This service allows you to read and update your default as well as subscribed Calendars. Using GAS, you can create Calendar events, and invite your friends programmatically. You can even grab event details and populate them in Sheets.

Creating Calendar events from a simple description

You can create an event by just passing a description as an argument to the createEventFromDescription method of the CalendarApp class:

```
function createCalendarEventFromDescription(){
  CalendarApp.getDefaultCalendar()
```

```
     .createEventFromDescription('Team Meeting,
        Monday from 3 PM to 4 PM');
}
```

Creating simple Calendar events

You can also create events by specifying the title, start time, and end time:

```
function createCalendarEvents() {
    var title = "Title of the event";
    var startTime = new Date("October 21, 2015 21:00:00");
    var endTime = new Date("October 21, 2015 21:30:00");

    CalendarApp.getDefaultCalendar()
       .createEvent(title, startTime, endTime);
}
```

Creating events with options

The following code shows how to create an event with the specified options, such as the description and location. Uncomment the sendInvites line only if you insert the guest's e-mail ID(s). Use a comma to separate them if there is more than one e-mail ID:

```
function createCalendarEventsWithOptions() {
  var options = {
    description : 'Description of the event',
    location : 'Event Location',
    //sendInvites : true,
    //guests : 'Comma-separated list of guest email IDs.'
  };

  var title = "Title of the event";
  var startTime = new Date("October 21, 2015 21:00:00");
  var endTime = new Date("October 21, 2015 21:30:00");

  CalendarApp.getDefaultCalendar()
     .createEvent(title, startTime, endTime, options);
}
```

Creating events from Sheets data

To create events from prepopulated Sheets data, create a Sheet named `Events` and create column headers as shown here:

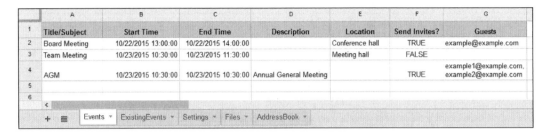

	A	B	C	D	E	F	G
1	Title/Subject	Start Time	End Time	Description	Location	Send Invites?	Guests
2	Board Meeting	10/22/2015 13:00:00	10/22/2015 14:00:00		Conference hall	TRUE	example@example.com
3	Team Meeting	10/23/2015 10:30:00	10/23/2015 11:30:00		Meeting hall	FALSE	
4	AGM	10/23/2015 10:30:00	10/23/2015 10:30:00	Annual General Meeting		TRUE	example1@example.com, example2@example.com
5							
6							

Events ▾ ExistingEvents ▾ Settings ▾ Files ▾ AddressBook ▾

Create the function `createCalendarEventsFromSheetData` as shown here:

```
function createCalendarEventsFromSheetData() {
  /*
   * 'Events' sheet column numbers,
   * use 0 for column 'A',
   * 1 for column 'B' and so on.
   * This makes life easy to use in '0' indexed JS arrays.
   *
   */
  const TITLE = 0;
  const START_TIME = 1;
  const END_TIME = 2;
  const DESCRIPTION = 3;
  const LOCATION = 4;
  const SEND_INVITES = 5;
  const GUESTS = 6;

  var sheet = SpreadsheetApp.getActiveSpreadsheet()
            .getSheetByName("Events");

  var data = sheet.getDataRange().getValues();

  // Remove header
  var header = data.shift();

  var options = {
    description : '',
    location : '',
```

```
    sendInvites : false,
    guests : ''
  };

  for(var i in data){
    /*
     * 'data' is a 2-dim array.
     * First index for row numbers and
     * second index for column numbers.
     *
     */
    options.description = data[i][DESCRIPTION];
    options.location = data[i][LOCATION];
    options.sendInvites = data[i][SEND_INVITES];
    options.guests = data[i][GUESTS];

    var title = data[i][TITLE];
    var startTime = data[i][START_TIME];
    var endTime = data[i][END_TIME];

    CalendarApp.getDefaultCalendar()
      .createEvent(title, startTime, endTime, options);
  }
}
```

Creating events from an external CSV file's contents

Instead of creating events from Sheet data, you can create them from an external CSV file uploaded to the Drive. Upload a CSV file with the same headers as in the previous task.

Get the key/ID of the uploaded file and replace it with the following code:

```
function createEventsFromCsvData(){
  // CSV columns, 0 based.
  const TITLE = 0;
  const START_TIME = 1;
  const END_TIME = 2;
  const DESCRIPTION = 3;
  const LOCATION = 4;
  const SEND_INVITES = 5;
  const GUESTS = 6;
```

```
// Put the key/ID of the CSV file placed in Drive.
var blob = DriveApp.getFileById("[[ CSV file id ]]").getBlob();
var str = blob.getDataAsString();

var data = Utilities.parseCsv(str);
// Now the data is a two-dimensional array

// Remove header
data.shift();

var options = {
  description : '',
  location : '',
  sendInvites : false,
  guests : ''
};

for(var i in data){

  // Skip if no title
  if(!data[i][0]) continue;

  // Populate the options object
  options.description = data[i][DESCRIPTION];
  options.location = data[i][LOCATION];
  options.sendInvites = data[i][SEND_INVITES];
  options.guests = data[i][GUESTS];

  var title = data[i][TITLE];
  var startTime = data[i][START_TIME];
  var endTime = data[i][END_TIME];

  CalendarApp.getDefaultCalendar()
    .createEvent(title, startTime, endTime, options);

  }
}
```

Enabling advanced Google services

Until now, you have been using GAS's basic services, such as `GmailApp` and `ContactsApp`. Now it is time to learn how to enable advanced services.

In this task, we are going to use a Calendar service, which is an advanced service, so we have to enable it before using it.

In the script editor, click on **Resources**, and then on **Advanced Google services...**, and a pop-up window will open:

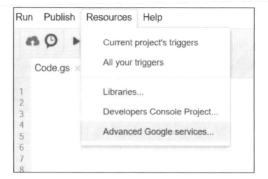

In the **Advanced Google Services** pop-up window, all the GAS advanced services will be listed. Look for the **Calendar API** service, select the latest version (it is selected by default), and then enable it if is not already enabled. In the following screenshot, you can see that the Calendar API service is enabled:

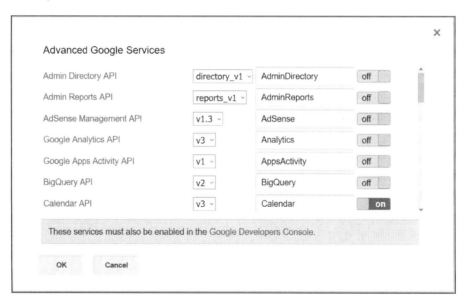

Enabling advanced services only in scripts is not enough, you also need to enable it in the Google Developers Console, as indicated in the pop-up window. To do so, click on the link provided in the pop-window.

Then a new browser window or tab will open with popular APIs listed as groups. You can see **Calendar API** under the **Google Apps APIs** group. If not listed, search the word `calendar` using the search option provided at the top of the page.

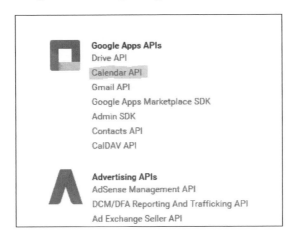

Click on **Calendar API** (highlighted in yellow in the preceding screenshot), then on the follow-up web page, click on **Enable API**:

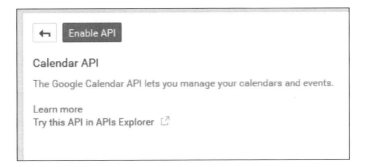

That's all; you have enabled Calendar advanced services.

Listing all the Calendars

After enabling Calendar advanced services, you can use the `listCalendars` function to log all of your Calendars:

```
/**
 *  Logs all of your calendars with IDs.
 *
 */
function listCalendars() {
  var calendars, pageToken = null;

  do {
    calendars = Calendar.CalendarList.list({
      maxResults: 100,
      pageToken: pageToken
    });

    if (calendars.items && calendars.items.length > 0) {
      for (var i = 0; i < calendars.items.length; i++) {
        var calendar = calendars.items[i];
        Logger.log('%s (ID: %s)', calendar.summary, calendar.id);
      }
    } else {
      Logger.log('No calendars found.');
    };

    // If more than one page, then return a token, else null.
    pageToken = calendars.nextPageToken;

  } while (pageToken);
}
```

The `Calendar.CalendarList.list` object returns a list of all the Calendars, provided that the number of Calendars is less than the value of `maxResults`. If the number of Calendars is greater than this value, then the `nextPageToken` value is used as a page token for the next iteration. A sample output of the log is shown here:

```
Logs                                                              ×

[15-10-23 09:21:48:965 PDT] graam.odesk@gmail.com (ID: graam.odesk@gmail.com)
[15-10-23 09:21:48:966 PDT] raamalingamg@gmail.com (ID: raamalingamg@gmail.com)
[15-10-23 09:21:48:966 PDT] Destination (ID:
0sb6c063gl24270vanm17efv40@group.calendar.google.com)
[15-10-23 09:21:48:967 PDT] Source (ID:
gjk6d3cn0t213uea60mnacdi8o@group.calendar.google.com)
[15-10-23 09:21:48:968 PDT] Birthdays (ID: #contacts@group.v.calendar.google.com)
[15-10-23 09:21:48:968 PDT] Holidays in India (ID: en.indian#holiday@group.v.calendar.google.com)
[15-10-23 09:21:48:969 PDT] Holidays in United States (ID:
en.usa#holiday@group.v.calendar.google.com)




    OK
```

Listing Calendar events in Sheets

To list events from any one Calendar into Sheets, create a new Sheet named
ExistingEvents and add the following function:

```
function listEventsFromOneCalendar() {
  var sheet = SpreadsheetApp.getActiveSpreadsheet()
       .getSheetByName("ExistingEvents");

  var source = "Replace with source calendar email id";
  var srcCalId = Calendar.Calendars.get(source).id;

  var syncdays = 30;
  var now = new Date();
  var min = new Date(now.getFullYear(), now.getMonth(),
     now.getDate());
  var max = new Date(now.getFullYear(), now.getMonth(),
     now.getDate() + syncdays);

  var srcEvents = Calendar.Events.list(srcCalId, {
    timeMin: min.toISOString(),
    timeMax: max.toISOString(),
```

```
    singleEvents: true,
    orderBy: 'startTime',
}).items;

/*
 * To store events data in a spreadsheet we need
 * to construct a 2-dim array
 *
 */
var output = [];

/*
 * 'srcEvents' is an array of event objects.
 *
 * Every event object is passed as 'e' to the anonymous
 * function.
 *
 */
srcEvents.forEach(function(e){
  // Construct an event array (1-dim)
  var event = [];

  /*
   * Returns "" if object value is 'null' or 'undefined'
   *    otherwise returns the object value.
   *
   */
  event.push(e.summary || "");
  event.push(e.start.dateTime || "");
  event.push(e.end.dateTime || "");
  event.push(e.description || "");
  event.push(e.location || "");

  // Push each event array to output (2-dim array).
  output.push(event);
});

var header = [
              "Title/Subject",
              "Start Time",
              "End Time",
              "Description",
              "Location"
```

```
            ];

    // Insert header at the top of the output.
    output.unshift(header);

    sheet.clearContents();

    sheet.getRange(1, 1, output.length, header.length)
    .setValues(output);
  };
```

The function we just mentioned collects all the events from the Calendar, constructs a 2-dimensional array, and stores that array in the `ExistingEvents` sheet. A sample output of the preceding code is shown here:

	A	B	C	D	E	F
1	Title/Subject	Start Time	End Time	Description	Location	
2	Board Meeting	2015-10-22T13:00:00+05:30	2015-10-22T14:00:00+05:30		Conference hall	
3	AGM	2015-10-23T10:30:00+05:30	2015-10-23T10:30:00+05:30	Annual General Meeting		
4	Team Meeting	2015-10-23T10:30:00+05:30	2015-10-23T11:30:00+05:30		Meeting hall	
5						
6						
7						

Events ▾ ExistingEvents ▾ Settings ▾ Files ▾ AddressBook ▾

Syncing events from one Calendar to another Calendar

The `syncEvents` function (listed in the following code) syncs the last 30 days events from the source Calendar to the destination Calendar. To test this application, create the main function `syncEvents` and other helper functions such as `updateEvent_`, `deleteEvent_`, and `insertEvent_`. We are marking those events synced from the source to the destination by prefixing `sync:` and enclosing an event title/summary in square brackets. For example, if the source event is `Example event`, then it will be marked as `[sync:Example event]` and inserted/updated in the destination Calendar:

```
/**
 * Replace Source and Destination with your own Calendars name.
 *
 * You should have write access in the destination Calendar,
 * in other words it should have been created by you.
 *
 */
```

```
function syncEvents() {
  const RATE_LIMIT = 10; // Milliseconds

  var source = "[[ Source ]]"; // Source calendar email id.
  var destination = "Destination"; // Destination calendar name.

  var srcCalId = Calendar.Calendars.get(source).id;

  // Returns calendars (matching with the name) as an array
  var dstCal = CalendarApp
                .getCalendarsByName(destination)[0];

  var dstCalId = dstCal.getId();

  var syncdays = 30;
  var now = new Date();

  var min = new Date(now.getFullYear(), now.getMonth(),
  now.getDate());
  var max = new Date(now.getFullYear(), now.getMonth(),
  now.getDate() + syncdays);

  // Get all source events as an array of objects.
  var srcEvents = Calendar.Events.list(srcCalId, {
    timeMin: min.toISOString(),
    timeMax: max.toISOString(),
    singleEvents: true,
    orderBy: 'startTime',
  }).items;

  // Get all destination events as an array of objects.
  var allDstEvents = Calendar.Events.list(dstCalId, {
    timeMin: min.toISOString(),
    timeMax: max.toISOString(),
    singleEvents: true,
    orderBy: 'startTime',
  }).items;

  /*
   * Get all destination events already synced from source
   * identified with the help of prefix '[sync:'
   *
   */
  var dstEvents = allDstEvents.filter(function(event){
      return /\[sync:\w+/.test(event.summary)?true:false;
```

```
  });

  // UPDATE all dstEvents with the corresponding srcEvents.
  for(var d in dstEvents){
    for(var s in srcEvents){

      if(dstEvents[d] && srcEvents[s] && dstEvents[d].id ==
      srcEvents[s].id){
        /*
         * Update srcEvents with 'sync:' marking in the
         * destination calendar.
         *
         */
        srcEvents[s].summary = srcEvents[s].summary||'' + "
        [sync:"+source+"]";

        updateEvent_(srcEvents[s],dstCalId);

        // Delete updated dstEvents and srcEvents.
        srcEvents.splice(s,1);
        dstEvents.splice(d,1);
        Utilities.sleep(RATE_LIMIT);
      }

    }
  };

  /*
   * DELETE remaining dstEvents (those that do not exist in
   * srcEvents).
   *
   */
  for(var d in dstEvents){
    deleteEvent_(dstEvents[d],dstCalId);
    Utilities.sleep(RATE_LIMIT);
  };

  // INSERT remaining srcEvents (those do not exist in dstEvents).
  for(var s in srcEvents){
    srcEvents[s].summary = srcEvents[s].summary||''
+ " [sync:"+source+"]";
    insertEvent_(srcEvents[s],dstCalId);
    Utilities.sleep(RATE_LIMIT);
  }
};
```

The previously mentioned `syncEvents` function collects events from the `Source` and `Destination` events and processes them as follows:

- It updates all the events that appear in both the source and destination (common to both arrays)
- It deletes all the events that are not present in the source but are present in the destination (that is, they are present in the destination only)
- It inserts all the events that appear in the source but not in the destination (that is, they are present in the source only)

The helper functions are listed here:

```
function updateEvent_(evt,calId){
  Calendar.Events.update( evt, calId, evt.id );
};


function deleteEvent_(evt,calId){
  Calendar.Events.remove(calId, evt.id);
};


function insertEvent_(evt,calId){
  try{
    Calendar.Events.insert(evt, calId);
  } catch(e) {
    var err = e.message;
    var newEvt = {
      summary:evt.summary,
      start:evt.start,
      end:evt.end,
      attachments:evt.attachments,
      attendees:evt.attendees,
      reminders:evt.reminders
    };

    if(err.search(/identifier already exists/gi) >= 0){
      updateEvent_(evt,calId);
    } else if(err.search(/Not Found/gi) >= 0){
      insertEvent_(newEvt,calId);
    } else if(err.search(/Invalid resource/gi) >= 0){
      insertEvent_(newEvt,calId);
    } else {
```

```
        Logger.log("%s [%s]\n",evt,err);
      };
    }
  };
```

Congratulations! You have created a working Calendar sync application.

The DriveApp class

This class allows you to create, search, and modify files and folders in your Drive.

For reference documentation on the `DriveApp` class, refer to the website: `https://developers.google.com/apps-script/reference/drive/drive-app?hl=en`.

Creating customized PDF files

Imagine that you need to create customized PDF files from the Sheet or external data. We can create PDF files from the HTML template. You simply need to format column headers and put some sample data in a new Sheet (`AddressBook`) as shown in the following screenshot:

	A	B	C	D	E	F
1	Name	Title	Company	Address	City	St. Zip / Pin Code
2	Aaron	Secretary	ABC Company	123, 1st Stree	City 1	123456
3	Stephen	Manager	ABC Company	123, 1st Stree	City 2	123456
4	Francis	Co-Ordinator	ABC Company	123, 1st Stree	City 3	123456
5	Robert	Clerk	XYZ Company	123, 1st Stree	City 4	123456
6	John	Director	XYZ Company	123, 1st Stree	City 5	123456
7	Paul	President	XYZ Company	123, 1st Stree	City 6	123456
8						
9						

+ ≡ Settings ▾ Files ▾ AddressBook ◀ ▶

Create the `createPdfs` function in the `Code.gs` file as listed here:

```
function createPdfs(){

  // 0 based column numbers
  const NAME = 0;
  const TITLE = 1;
  const COMPANY = 2;
  const ADDRESS = 3;
```

```
const CITY = 4;
const ZIP_PIN = 5;


/* Get data from the sheet */
var sheet = SpreadsheetApp.getActiveSheet();
var data = sheet.getDataRange().getValues();
/*
 * Alternatively you can get data
 * from an external CSV file or anything else.
 *
 * Example:
 * var blob = DriveApp.getFileById(id).getBlob();
 * var text = blob.getDataAsString();
 * var data = JSON.parse(text);
 *
 */

// Remove headers
data.shift();

var folderName = "Letters";
var folder, folders = DriveApp.getFoldersByName(folderName);

// 'folders' is an iterator
if (folders.hasNext()){
  // Get first folder if more than 1 with same name.
  folder = folders.next();
} else {
  // Create folder if it does not exist.
  folder = DriveApp.createFolder(folderName);
}

for(var i in data){
  /*
   * Set as global variables so that we will be able to access
   * in the Template.html code.
   *
   */
  name = data[i][NAME];
  title = data[i][TITLE];
  company = data[i][COMPANY];
  address = data[i][ADDRESS];
```

```
    city = data[i][CITY];
    zip_pin = data[i][ZIP_PIN];

    var html =
    HtmlService.createTemplateFromFile
    ("Template.html").evaluate();

    // Convert HTML to PDF
    var pdf = html.getAs("application/pdf")
.setName(name + ".pdf");

    // Save in the 'My Drive | Letter' folder.
    folder.createFile(pdf);
  }


}
```

The `createPdfs` function gets data from a Sheet, or you can modify it to get data from an external source. It creates an HTML template for each row of data, converts it to a PDF, and stores it in a Drive folder. Let's assign the `name`, `title`, `company`, `address`, `city`, and `zip_pin` variables as global variables. Only then can we get those values in an HTML template.

Create an HTML file called `Template.html` and enter the code listed here:

```html
<!DOCTYPE html>
<html>
  <body>
    <p>To</p>
    <p>
      <?= name ?><br />
      <?= title ?><br />
      <?= company ?><br />
      <?= address ?><br />
      <?= city ?><br />
      <?= zip_pin ?><br />
    </p>
    <p> </p>
    <p>Dear <?= name ?>,</p>
    <p>Your message goes here...</p>

    <p>Regards,<br />[Your name]</p>
  </body>
</html>
```

This code gets the global variable values as we described and returns customized HTML. Update your message and name in the appropriate places. From this HTML template, the `createPdfs` function creates PDF files, each of which is customized with individual row data from the Sheet. All the PDF files created are saved in Drive (`My Drive | Letter`) folder.

The content of one of the PDF files (`Aaron.pdf`) created as per the Sheet data (row 2) is shown in the following screenshot:

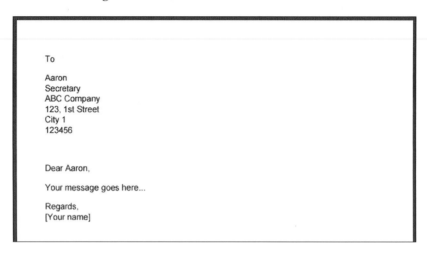

For a sample, we used this template for a simple letter, but you can use any type of template, such as an invoice, resume, job application, and more, as per your requirements and imagination.

Creating a Drive file routing application

This application can move files by matching the name with the criteria terms in the `Settings` tab. First of all, create a new Sheet or tab named `Settings` and column headings as shown here:

	A	B
1	In root folder, if filename contains	then move to this folder
2	Apple	Fruits
3	Cat	Animals
4	Brinjal	Vegetables
5		
6		
7		
8		

Also, create the `moveDriveFiles` function as shown in the following code snippet. If you run this function, then it moves files from the root folder to the appropriate folder as per the settings in the **Settings** Sheet. The destination folder is created if it does not already exist. You can also create a trigger to run this function at a predefined time or periodically:

```
function moveDriveFiles(){
  var SheetSettings = SpreadsheetApp.getActiveSpreadsheet()
        .getSheetByName("Settings");

  // Open the root folder.
  var rootFolderName = "Replace with root folder name.";
  var rootFolder, destFolder, folders = DriveApp
        .getFoldersByName(rootFolderName);

  // 'folders' is an iterator
  if (folders.hasNext()) rootFolder = folders.next();
  else {
    // Show warning "Folder does not exist."
    Browser.msgBox(
      "The root folder " + rootFolderName + " not exist."
    );

    return;
  }

  var data = SheetSettings.getDataRange().getValues();
  data.shift();// Remove header row

  for(var i in data){
    var fileName = data[i][0];
    var folderName = data[i][1];

    // Open or create the destination folder
    folders = rootFolder.getFoldersByName(folderName);

    if (folders.hasNext()) destFolder = folders.next();
    else destFolder = rootFolder.createFolder(folderName);

    /*
     * Move matching files to the destination folder
     * The filename should be enclosed in quotes.
     *
     */
    var dest, file, files = rootFolder
          .searchFiles('title contains "' + fileName + '"');
    /*
```

```
      * In the above line, the searchFiles method's argument should
      * be a string (SQL-like query), so take care to escape special
      * characters.
      * Here is an alternative way to write the method:
      * searchFiles("title contains \"" + fileName + "\"")
      *
      */


    /*
     * We cannot move files directly,
     * so copy file to the destination and remove in source.
     *
     */
    while (files.hasNext()){
      dest = destFolder;
      file = files.next();

      file.makeCopy(file, dest);
      rootFolder.removeFile(file);
    }
  }
}
```

Creating a Drive file search application

Now you are going to create a file search application. It can search files in Drive
with certain criteria in a text field. Create the functions onOpen, showSidebar,
and listDriveFiles in the Code.gs file as listed here:

```
function onOpen(){
  SpreadsheetApp.getUi().createAddonMenu()
  .addItem("File Search", "showSidebar")
  .addToUi();
  showSidebar();
}

/**
 * Opens sidebar containing the user interface.
 *
 */
function showSidebar() {
  SpreadsheetApp.getUi().showSidebar(
    HtmlService.createHtmlOutputFromFile('Sidebar')
      .setTitle('Search Files in Drive')
  );
}
```

The onOpen function creates an add-ons menu and calls the showSidebar function. This means whenever the spreadsheet is opened, the add-ons menu is added and the sidebar is displayed:

```
/**
 *  Lists files matching with arg 'txt', in the Settings sheet.
 *
 */
function listDriveFiles(txt){
  // 'Files' sheet column heading.
  var header = ["File", "URL"];

  var output = [header];

  var file, files = DriveApp.searchFiles
  ('title contains "' + txt + '"');

  // 'files' is an iterator.
  while (files.hasNext()){
    file = files.next();
    var name = file.getName();
    var link = file.getUrl();

    output.push([name,link]);
  };

  var sheet = SpreadsheetApp.getActiveSpreadsheet()
        .getSheetByName("Files");

  sheet.clearContents();

  /*
   * output.length for number of rows and
   * header.length for number of columns
   *
   */
  sheet.getRange(1, 1, output.length, header.length)
    .setValues(output);
}
```

Create a new HTML file named `Sidebar.html` and put the following code in it:

```html
<!DOCTYPE html>
<html>
  <head>
    <base target="_top">
    <link rel="stylesheet"
     href="https://ssl.gstatic.com/docs/script
     /css/add-ons1.css" />
    <script
     src="//ajax.googleapis.com/ajax/libs/jquery/
     1.9.1/jquery.min.js">
    </script>

  </head>

  <body>
    <input type="text" id="txt" />
    <button class="green" id="btn">Search</button>
  </body>

  <script>
    // On document load, assign click handler to the search
    // button.
    $(function() {
      $('#btn').click(listFiles);
    });

    function listFiles() {
      this.disabled = true;
      $('#error,#success').remove();
      google.script.run
        .withSuccessHandler(function(msg,elm){
          elm.disabled = false;
        })
        .withFailureHandler(function(err,elm){
          elm.disabled = false;
          showError(err,elm);
        })
        .withUserObject(this)
```

```
        .listDriveFiles($('#txt').val());
}

/**
 * Inserts a div that contains success message after a given
 * element.
 *
 * @param {string} msg - The message to display.
 * @param {object} element - The element after which to
 * display the message.
 *
 */
function showSuccess(msg,element) {
  var div = $('<div id="success"><font color="green">'
  + msg + '</font></div>');
  $(element).after(div);
}

/**
 * Inserts a div that contains error message after a given
 * element.
 *
 * @param {string} msg - The error message to display.
 * @param {object} element - The element after which to
 *  display the error.
 *
 */
function showError(msg, element) {
  var div = $('<div id="error" class="error">'
  + msg + '</div>');
  $(element).after(div);
}

  </script>
</html>
```

On opening the spreadsheet or running the showSidebar function, the sidebar opens as shown in the following screenshot, except the text Chapter in the text field. You can type any other text to search files. On clicking the **Search** button, the script searches the Drive for those files whose name contains the text and populates data in the Files Sheet.

The following screenshot shows the sidebar and sample output:

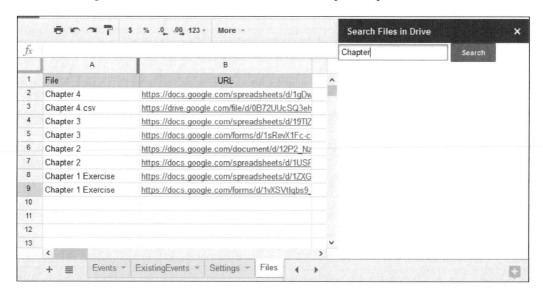

Summary

In this chapter, you learned about, and created, many useful real-world applications, including an event sync application. In the next chapter, you will learn how to create RSS/Atom readers and language translator applications.

6
Creating Feed Reader and Translator Applications

In the previous chapter, you learned to create Calendar events and Drive applications. You built many real-world applications.

In this chapter, you will learn to

- Create a Google search
- Create a stock quote ticker
- Create an RSS feed reader
- Create an Atom feed reader
- Create a language translator application
- Creating a document reviewing and instant inline commenting application

The UrlFetchApp class

The UrlFetchApp class can be used to issue HTTP/HTTPS request and get responses to/from any websites/URL. For example, the UrlFetchApp.fetch ("https://ajax.googleapis.com/ajax/services/search/web?v=1.0&q=PACKT") code returns the search result with the search term PACKT. The response will be a raw content along with HTTP headers.

If the communication between the UrlFetchApp class's fetch method and the URL is okay then the URL should return a response code 200. Otherwise, any other number corresponds to the type of error. We can check the response code before proceeding further using the getResponseCode method.

You can get the content text using the `getContentText` method and parsing it to JSON objects. The following code snippet pulls the content text and parses to JSON:

```
var url = "https://ajax.googleapis.com/ajax/services/search
/web?v=1.0&q=PACKT";
try{
    var resp = UrlFetchApp.fetch(url);
    if(resp.getResponseCode() == 200){
      var text = resp.getContentText();
      var json = JSON.parse(text);
      Logger.log(json);
    }
  } catch(e){
    Logger.log(e);
  };
```

For your understanding the logged output is furnished here (text might be truncated and formatted for brevity):

```
{
  responseDetails=null,
  responseData={
    cursor={
      moreResultsUrl=http://www.google.com/search?oe=utf8&ie=utf8
        &source=uds&start=0&hl=en&q=PACKT,
      resultCount=800,000,
      pages=[{start=0, label=1}, {start=4, label=2}, {start=8,
        label=3}, {start=12, label=4}, {start=16, label=5},
        {start=20, label=6}, {start=24, label=7}, {start=28,
        label=8}],
      searchResultTime=0.29,
      currentPageIndex=0,
      estimatedResultCount=800000
    },
    results=[
      {
        visibleUrl=www.packtpub.com,
        cacheUrl=http://www.google.com/search?q=cache:rbL6l6pFt8…,
        GsearchResultClass=GwebSearch,
        title=<b>Packt</b> Publishing | Technology Books, eBook…,
        titleNoFormatting=Packt Publishing | Technology Books…,
        url=https://www.packtpub.com/,
        content=<b>Packt</b> Publishing is the leading UK provid…,
        unescapedUrl=https://www.packtpub.com/
```

```
    }, {
        visibleUrl=www.packtpub.com,
        cacheUrl=http://www.google.com/search?q=cache:wo2TeIpsCG…,
        GsearchResultClass=GwebSearch,
        title=Free Learning | <b>PACKT</b> Books - <b>Packt</b> …,
        titleNoFormatting=Free Learning | PACKT Books - Packt Pu…,
        url=https://www.packtpub.com/packt/offers/free-learning,
        content=A new free programming tutorial book every day...,
    }, {
        visibleUrl=www.packtpub.com,
        cacheUrl=http://www.google.com/search?q=cache:D7qMTpx1Nu…,
        GsearchResultClass=GwebSearch,
        title=All Books and eBooks | <b>PACKT</b> Books - <b>Pac…,
        titleNoFormatting=All Books and eBooks | PACKT Books - P…,
        url=https://www.packtpub.com/all,
        content=Packt Publishing provides technology eBooks, boo…,
        unescapedUrl=https://www.packtpub.com/all
    }
  ]
 },
 responseStatus=200
}
```

The top-level objects of the JSON are `responseDetails`, `responseData`, and `responseStatus`. If Google has returned the correct response, then the `responseStatus` value should be `200`. This is returned by the Google search service not the `UrlFetchApp` status. You can also check whether the `responseStatus` value equals to `200` or not, to confirm if the response content is okay.

You need to dig into the `responseData` object, which contains the result as an array of object. To get the array, use `json.responseData.results` and then cycle through the array to get the required result data. We will create an application to search Google and to populate the result in Sheet.

Creating a Google search application

Create a new Sheet, rename it as `Google` and create headers as shown in the following screenshot:

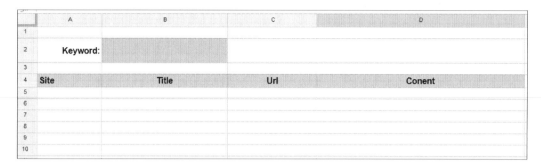

Then, enter the following code in the `Code.gs` file:

```
function searchGoogle(){

    var ss = SpreadsheetApp.getActiveSpreadsheet();
    var SheetGoogle = ss.getSheetByName("Google");
    var kwd = SheetGoogle.getRange("B2").getValue();

    // Encode URI components if any in kwd
    kwd = encodeURIComponent(kwd);

    // Replace space with '+'
    kwd = kwd.replace(/%20/gi, "+");

    // Remove '?' marks
    kwd = kwd.replace(/%3F/gi, "");

    var url =
    "https://ajax.googleapis.com/ajax/services/
    search/web?v=3.0&q=" + kwd;

    try{
      var resp = UrlFetchApp.fetch(url).getContentText();
      var json = JSON.parse(resp);
      var result = json.responseData.results;
    } catch(e){
      Logger.log(e);
    };
```

```
// We require a 2-dimensional array to store data in sheet
var output = [];
var visibleUrl,title,url,content;

for(var i=0; i<result.length; i++){
  visibleUrl = result[i].visibleUrl;
  title = result[i].title;
  url = result[i].url;
  content = result[i].content;

  output.push([visibleUrl,title,url,content]);
};

/*
 * output.length for number of rows and output[0].length for
 * number of columns
 *
 */
SheetGoogle.getRange(5, 1, output.length, output[0].length)
  .setValues(output);
}
```

A sample output of the application is shown in the following screenshot:

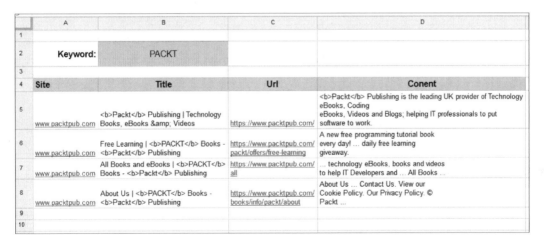

You can test the code using other keywords in cell *B2*. You can create a button or custom menu for the `searchGoogle` function, so that you can search frequently.

Creating a stock quote ticker application

A simple function to get stock quotes from Google Finance is shown in the following screenshot. The query string (q) specifies NASDAQ as the stock exchange and GOOG (Google) as the scrip name.

```
function getStockQuote1(){
  var url =
  "http://finance.google.com/finance/info?q=NASDAQ:GOOG";

  var resp = UrlFetchApp.fetch(url).getContentText();
  Logger.log(resp);
}
```

In the preceding code, we are using the UrlFetchApp class's fetch method. The logged response is as follows:

```
// [
{
"id": "304466804484872"
,"t" : "GOOG"
,"e" : "NASDAQ"
,"l" : "717.00"
,"l_fix" : "717.00"
,"l_cur" : "717.00"
,"s": "0"
,"ltt":"4:00PM EST"
,"lt" : "Nov 13, 4:00PM EST"
,"lt_dts" : "2015-11-13T16:00:01Z"
,"c" : "-14.23"
,"c_fix" : "-14.23"
,"cp" : "-1.95"
,"cp_fix" : "-1.95"
,"ccol" : "chr"
,"pcls_fix" : "731.23"
}
]
```

In the returned response text, you can see that the first four characters are a line break, two slashes (//), and a space character, so you have to remove them before parsing the required JSON object. Striping out the first four characters from the returned string makes things easier. You can use the substr method to strip the first four characters. The parse method of JavaScript JSON (JavaScript Object Notation) object parses the string to the JSON object.

The modified code to retrieve **Last Traded Price (LTP)** of Google scrip is:

```
function getStockQuote2(){
  var url =
  "http://finance.google.com/finance/info?q=NASDAQ:GOOG";

  var resp = UrlFetchApp.fetch(url).getContentText().substr(4);
  var json = JSON.parse(resp);
  Logger.log(json[0].l);
}
```

You can use multiple scrips (comma separated) in the query string. For example, `http://finance.google.com/finance/info?q=NASDAQ:GOOG,AMD,MCHP`. Then, the response would be an array of stock quote objects. You will have to cycle through the array to get each scrip data.

We will create a complete working stock quote application. Create or add a new Sheet and rename it as `Quotes`, populate the SYMBOL column, and format it as shown here:

	A	B	C
1	SYMBOL	PRICE	TRADED TIME
2	GOOG		
3	AMD		
4	MCHP		
5	INTC		
6	LHCG		
7			
8			

Edit the `getStockQuotes` function in the `Code.gs` file as listed here:

```
function getStockQuotes(){
  var SheetQuotes = SpreadsheetApp.getActiveSpreadsheet()
                  .getSheetByName("Quotes");

  var data = SheetQuotes.getDataRange().getValues();

  // Remove the header from data.
  var header = data.shift();

  // Extracts all symbols from sheet data.
  var aScrips = [];
  for(var i in data) aScrips.push(data[i][0]);

  // Join all scrip names with comma.
  var sScrips = aScrips.join(",");
```

```
// Fetch data with scrip names as query.
var url =
"http://finance.google.com/finance/info?q=NASDAQ:"+sScrips;

// Send the request to the url
try{
  var resp = UrlFetchApp.fetch(url).getContentText().substr(4);
  var json = JSON.parse(resp);
} catch (e) {
  Logger.log(e.message);
  return;
}

// We require a 2-dimensional array to store data in sheet.
var output = [];

// Traverse through all JSON objects.
for(var i in json){
  var q = json[i];

  // Symbol, price and traded time.
  output.push([q.t,q.l,q.ltt]);
};

// Restore the header again.
output.unshift(header);

// Save the output in sheet.
SheetQuotes.getDataRange().setValues(output);
}
```

The following is a sample output of the application:

	A	B	C	D
1	SYMBOL	PRICE	TRADED TIME	
2	GOOG	717	4:00PM EST	
3	AMD	1.99	4:00PM EST	
4	MCHP	45.64	4:00PM EST	
5	INTC	32.11	4:00PM EST	
6	LHCG	46.17	4:00PM EST	
7				
8				

For a repeated quote tick, you can create a minutes trigger for the `getStockQuotes` function.

Logging Bitcoin quotes

Have you ever heard about Bitcoin, digital, or virtual currency, and ever watched Bitcoin price ticks to buy/sell Bitcoins? **Bitcoin** is a digital asset and trending a new payment system spreading all over the world. Here is an interesting application to log real-time Bitcoin prices. In this application, we will log prices from the Bitstamp trading platform. `https://www.bitstamp.net` provides API to get Bitcoin real-time price ticks.

```
function getBitCoinPrice(){
  // BitStamp api url
  var url = "https://www.bitstamp.net/api/ticker/";

  var resp = UrlFetchApp.fetch(url);

  if(resp.getResponseCode() == 200){
    var json = JSON.parse(resp);
    Logger.log(json);
  }
}
```

The response from the Bitstamp API which is parsed as JSON is provided here:

```
{volume=6209.19457553, high=422.00, last=420.39, low=414.00,
vwap=419.15, ask=421.48, bid=420.23, open=421.15,
timestamp=1455894447}
```

The complete code to parse the said JSON objects to Sheet is provided here:

```
/**
 *  Log bitcoin price ticks in sheet
 *
 */
function getBitCoinData(){
  var ss = SpreadsheetApp.getActiveSpreadsheet();
  var SheetBitCoin = ss.getSheetByName("Bitcoin");

  // Header labels at the top row of the sheet.
  var header = [
      "Timestamp",
      "High",
      "Low",
      "Volume",
      "Bid",
      "Ask"
    ];
```

```
// Insert headers at the top row of the Bitcoin sheet.
SheetBitCoin.getRange(1,1,1,6).setValues([header]);
// setValues accept 2-dim array

// BitStamp api url
var url = "https://www.bitstamp.net/api/ticker/";

try{
  var resp = UrlFetchApp.fetch(url);

  // Proceed if no errors returned.
  if(resp.getResponseCode() == 200){

    var json = JSON.parse(resp);

    var output = [];

    /*
     * Bitstamp returns timestamp in seconds
     * (elapsed since epoch), but JavaScript Date accepts in
     * milliseconds, so multiply by 1000.
     *
     */
    output.push( new Date(json.timestamp *= 1000) );

    // last 24 hours high.
    output.push(json.high);

    // last 24 hours low.
    output.push(json.low);

    // last 24 hours volume.
    output.push(json.volume);

    // highest buy order.
    output.push(json.bid);

    // lowest sell order.
    output.push(json.ask);

    // Append output to Bitcoin sheet.
    SheetBitCoin.appendRow(output);
  }
```

```
    } catch(e){
      // Log errors to examine and debug it later.
      Logger.log(e);

      throw e;
    }
  };
```

A sample logged Bitcoin data is given here. The **High**, **Low**, and **Volume** values are the highest price, lowest price, and total volume in the last 24 hours. The **Bid** and **Ask** values are real-time values. Create a trigger for the repeated execution of the getBitCoinData function.

	A	B	C	D	E	F
1	Timestamp	High	Low	Volume	Bid	Ask
2	2/19/2016 22:11:37	422	414	6254.625033	418.56	419.94
3	2/19/2016 22:11:57	422	414	6254.983953	418.64	419.94
4	2/19/2016 22:12:48	422	414	6249.621827	418.89	419.94
5	2/19/2016 22:12:48	422	414	6249.621827	418.89	419.94
6	2/19/2016 22:13:01	422	414	6249.321827	418.95	419.94
7	2/19/2016 22:13:05	422	414	6249.321827	418.96	419.94
8	2/19/2016 22:14:02	422	414	6274.848596	419.2	419.94
9	2/19/2016 22:14:13	422	414	6273.421186	419.25	419.94
10	2/19/2016 22:14:17	422	414	6273.421186	419.26	419.94
11	2/19/2016 22:14:17	422	414	6273.421186	419.26	419.94
12						
13						
14						

RSS and Atom feeds

RSS stands for **Rich Site Summary**. It is used to publish frequently updated information. Users need standalone special software applications or browser add-ons called **RSS readers** to read information from any feeds.

Feed documents contain summarized or full text, metadata, publishing date, author name, and so on. Using feed, users can receive timely website updates or aggregate data from many websites. User need not check manually for any updates from those websites frequently, but subscribe for feeds. Feed reader checks the subscribed website frequently for any new data and retrieves them.

Skeleton of a RSS feed document

An example of a RSS feed document is listed here:

```
<?xml version="1.0" encoding="UTF-8"?>
<rss version="2.0">
  <channel>
    <title>Title of the channel</title>
    <description>A brief description of the channel</description>
    <language>en-US</language>
    <item>
      <title>Item title</title>
      <link>Link to the item</link>
      <pubDate>Fri, 30 Oct 2015 19:41:00 +0000</pubDate>
      <creator><![CDATA[Author Name]]></creator>
      <category><![CDATA[NEWS]]></category>
      <description><![CDATA[encoded description...]]></description>
    </item>
    <item> … </item>
    <item> … </item>
    <item> … </item>
  </channel>
</rss>
```

The first line specifies the version, as this one is an XML document, to the processing software application.

All other elements are enclosed within the rss root element.

The title, description, and language elements inside the channel element specify the title, description, and in which language the channel is published, respectively.

The item element is a repeated one, and it contains the individual feed item information, such as title (title of the item), link (link to the item), comments (comment about the item), pubDate (item published date), creator (creator of the item), category (specifying to which category the item belongs), description (a brief description about the item), and many more.

Creating an RSS reader application

You have to parse the required content from the XML document returned by
`UrlFetchApp` using `XmlService`. The actual code is furnished here:

```
function readRssFeedContents(){
  var SheetData = SpreadsheetApp.getActiveSpreadsheet()
                    .getSheets()[0];

  var title, posturl, author, row, output = [];

  // Prefix namespace.
  var dc =
  XmlService.getNamespace('http://purl.org/dc/elements/1.1/');

  // Fetch feed document.
  var xml = UrlFetchApp.fetch("http://siliconangle.com/feed/")
            .getContentText();

  // Parse the response text from the URL.
  var doc = XmlService.parse(xml);

  // Get child elements from the root element.
  var items = doc.getRootElement().getChild('channel')
            .getChildren('item');

  // Process the required data.
  for(var i=0; i<items.length; i++){
    title = items[i].getChild('title').getText();
    posturl = items[i].getChild('link').getText();
    author = items[i].getChild('creator', dc).getText();
    row = [title].concat(posturl, author);

    output.push(row);
  };

  // Write new data to sheet
  SheetData.getRange(2, 1, output.length, output[0].length)
    .setValues(output);
}
```

In the preceding code, `XmlService` is used to parse any well-structured XML content. In the mentioned sample source, we concentrated on `channel` elements and one or more `item` elements. The `item` element itself contains more information. To get the required data, you have to dig into the contents in the order of `channel` | `item` | `title` | `link` | `creator`. The `creator` element is prefixed with `dc`, so we have to assign the `dc` namespace URL at the top lines of the code.

A sample output of this application is shown here:

	Title	Post URL	Author
2	SXSW announces day-long online harassment summit in response to cancelled gaming sessions	http://siliconangle.com/blog/2015/10/30/sxsw-announces-day-long-online-harassment-summit-in-response-to-cancelled-gaming-sessions/	Eric David
3	PewDiePie says ad blockers are partly to blame for the creation of YouTube Red	http://siliconangle.com/blog/2015/10/30/pewdiepie-says-ad-blockers-are-partly-to-blame-for-the-creation-of-youtube-red/	Eric David
4	IndieCade co-chair John Sharp steps down, says the conference doesn't really help indie devs	http://siliconangle.com/blog/2015/10/30/indiecade-co-chair-john-sharp-steps-down-says-the-conference-doesnt-really-help-indie-devs/	Eric David
5	Digging up dark data: What puts IBM at the forefront of insight economy	#IBMinsight	http://siliconangle.com/blog/2015/10/30/ibm-is-at-the-forefront-of-insight-economy-ibminsight/	Heather Johnson
6	EA is betting heavily on the success of Star Wars Battlefront, raises 2016 outlook	http://siliconangle.com/blog/2015/10/30/ea-is-betting-heavily-on-the-success-of-star-wars-battlefront-raises-2016-outlook/	Eric David
7	How to avoid Uber's price surges	http://siliconangle.com/blog/2015/10/30/how-to-avoid-ubers-price-surges/	Mellisa Tolentino
8	Delivering on self-service analytics for all	#IBMinsight	http://siliconangle.com/blog/2015/10/30/delivering-on-self-service-analytics-for-all-ibminsight/	Andrew Ruggiero
9	Outcome-driven healthcare enabled by Watson, but security threats challenge	#IBMinsight	http://siliconangle.com/blog/2015/10/30/outcome-driven-healthcare-enabled-by-watson-but-security-threats-challenge-ibminsight/	Andrew Ruggiero
10	Microsoft's new Windows 10 preview build has some nice surprises including media casting	http://siliconangle.com/blog/2015/10/30/microsofts-new-windows-10-preview-build-has-some-nice-surprises-including-media-casting/	James Farrell
11	Step-by-step guide to add drawings to notes in Google Keep	http://siliconangle.com/blog/2015/10/30/step-by-step-guide-to-add-drawings-to-notes-in-google-keep/	Collen Kriel
12			
13			

Skeleton of an Atom feed document

Atom feeds are similar to RSS feeds with many advanced features. The `root` element is `feed` instead of `channel`. An example of an Atom feed document is shown here:

```xml
<?xml version="1.0" encoding="utf-8"?>
<feed xmlns="http://www.w3.org/2005/Atom">
  <title>Atom Feed</title>
  <subtitle>Subtitle of the feed</subtitle>
  <link href="http://example.com/" />
  <updated>2015-11-13T06:30:02Z</updated>
  <entry>
    <title>Title of the item</title>
    <link href="http://example.com" />
    <updated>2015-11-13T06:30:22Z</updated>
    <summary>Summary text of the item</summary>
    <author>
```

```
      <name>Author name</name>
      <email>example@example.com</email>
    </author>
  </entry>
  <entry>...</entry>
  <entry>...</entry>
  <entry>...</entry>
</feed>
```

Creating an Atom feed reader application

This application parses Google Hot Trends Atom Feed. The following is the code to read Google Trends Atom Feed content:

```
function readAtomFeedContents(){
  // SheetData refers left most sheet.
  var SheetData = SpreadsheetApp.getActiveSpreadsheet()
                  .getSheets()[0];

  // Set column titles.
  var title, description, output = [["Trends", "Related
  Searches"]];

  // Fetch data from the feed url.
  var xml = UrlFetchApp.fetch("http://www.google.com/trends/
  hottrends/atom/feed").getContentText();

  // Parse the result as xml content.
  var doc = XmlService.parse(xml);

  // Get item elements from the root element.
  var items = doc.getRootElement().getChild('channel')
          .getChildren('item');

  // Clear existing sheet data and sets new values.
  SheetData.clearContents();

  // Store new data.
  SheetData.getRange(1, 1, 1,output[0].length).setValues(output);

  /*
   * Dig into 'item' element and parse all the required data.
   * Get other related search terms.
   *
```

```
    */
for(var i=0; i<items.length; i++){
  title = items[i].getChild('title').getText();
  description = items[i].getChild('description').getText();
  output = [title].concat(description.split(','));

  // Sets output data in sheet.
  SheetData.getRange(i+2, 1, 1, output.length)
    .setValues([output]);
}
};
```

A sample output of the application is shown here:

	A	B	C	D
1	**Trends**	**Related Searches**		
2	All Saints Day			
3	When Does Daylight Saving Time End	Daylight Savings	daylight saving time	What Time Is It
4	Temple Football	Notre Dame	Temple Notre Dame	Temple
5	Time change			
6	JT Barrett	OVI		
7	Trick Or Treat Times 2015	Trick Or Treat Times		
8	Heidi Klum	Heidi Klum Halloween	Jessica Rabbit	Heidi Klum Halloween 2015
9	Georgia Bulldogs	Florida Georgia Game	Georgia Football	Georgia Florida Game
10	Time Change 2015 Fall			
11	Russian plane crash	it	plane crash	
12	NYC Marathon	Nyc Marathon Route	New York Marathon	
13	Iowa football	Iowa Hawkeyes		
14	Trick or Treat			
15	Ash vs Evil Dead	Evil Dead		
16	Golden State Warriors	Warriors		
17	Vampire Makeup			
18	Halloween Parade Nyc	NYC Halloween Parade		
19	Texas A&m Football			
20	Bartolo Colon			
21	Chipotle Halloween			
22				

Using optional parameters with the UrlFetchApp class

All foresaid applications fetch results from public URLs; this means that they do not require credentials. What if a website requires your credentials, such as username and password, before sending a response? You can provide credentials and other parameters as an optional parameter of the `UrlFetchApp` class, for example, `UrlFetchApp.fetch(url, params)`. The `params` parameter is similar to this:

```
var params = {
  method: "GET",
  headers: headers
}
```

The `headers` variable (the HTTP/HTTPS request headers) can be a JavaScript key/value map. You can provide your login credentials as headers:

```
var headers = {
  // Basic authentication
  Authorization: "Basic "
    + Utilities.base64Encode("username:password");
}
```

Your username and password will be encoded but not encrypted, so prefer HTTPS over HTTP.

> Not all websites support basic authentication; they mostly support OAuth. The `UrlFetchApp` class's built-in OAuth service is deprecated and moved to the open source library called the GAS library. More information on how to import the external library and use the OAuth2 open source library is provided in *Chapter 9, More Tips and Tricks and Creating an Add-on*.

The LanguageApp class

The `LanguageApp` class provides the `translate` method to translate any text from one language to another language.

For example, to translate `Google apps script for beginners` to French use the following code:

```
function translateToFrench(){
  var text = "Google apps script for beginners";
  var sourceLanguage = "en";
```

```
var targetLanguage = "fr";
var french = LanguageApp
   .translate(text, sourceLanguage, targetLanguage);

Logger.log(french);
}
```

The logged output would be: `Google Apps Script pour les débutants.`

 Google Translate service supports many languages. For more information on supported languages, visit:
`https://cloud.google.com/translate/v2/using_rest#language-params`

Creating the language translator application

This application translates text from one language to another. We will use one document as an origin/source document and the other one as a destination/target document. We are going to develop this application as an add-on. Although there is a built-in translate service available (in Docs application navigate to **Tools | Translate document...**), we have provided the language translator application to explore the capabilities of GAS.

Enter the following code in the source document's (Docs) `Code.gs` file:

```
/*
 * Replace with the id/key of the target document in which the
 * translated text to be saved.
 *
 */
var targetDocumentId = "Replace with target document id";
```

The preceding code sets the target document's ID to the `targetDocumentId` global variable. The target document is the document to which you are going to transfer the translated text. Replace the text within double quotes with the target document's ID as a string:

```
/**
 * Creates a menu entry in the Google Docs UI when the document
 * is opened.
 *
 */
function onOpen(e) {
```

```
    DocumentApp.getUi().createAddonMenu()
        .addItem('Start', 'showSidebar')
        .addToUi();
}
```

The preceding onOpen function creates an **Add-ons** menu with a menu item called **Start.** It is associated with the showSidebar function:

```
/**
 * Opens a sidebar in the document containing the add-on's user
 * interface.
 *
 */
function showSidebar() {
  var ui = HtmlService.createTemplateFromFile('Sidebar')
            .evaluate()
            .setTitle('Translate');

  DocumentApp.getUi().showSidebar(ui);
}
```

The preceding showSidebar function creates the sidebar with the required control elements.

```
/**
 * Gets the stored user preferences for the destination language,
 * if exist.
 *
 */
function getPreferences() {
  var userProperties = PropertiesService.getUserProperties();

  var languagePrefs = {
    destLang: userProperties.getProperty('destLang')
  };

  return languagePrefs;
};
```

The `getPreferences` function gets and returns the user's language preferences. The `runTranslation` function shown here translates the text from the source language to the destination language. The languages are notated by their two-letter short form. For example, English is `en`, German is `de`, and the default is auto, which means the Google Translate service will detect the source language itself. If the `savePrefs` argument is `true`, then the user language preference will be saved:

```
function runTranslation(dest, savePrefs) {
  if (savePrefs == true) {
    var userProperties = PropertiesService.getUserProperties();
    userProperties.setProperty('originLang', 'en');
    userProperties.setProperty('destLang', dest);
  }

  var srcFile = DocumentApp.getActiveDocument();
  var tgtFile = DocumentApp.openById(targetDocumentId);

  var srcBody = srcFile.getBody();
  var tgtBody = tgtFile.getBody();

  tgtBody.appendParagraph("");
  tgtBody.clear();

  var item = srcBody.getChild(0);

  while(item){
    var type = item.getType();

    if(type == "LIST_ITEM"){
      var attrib = item.getAttributes();
var srcText = item.getText();
var transText = LanguageApp.translate(srcText, "en", dest);
tgtBody.appendParagraph(transText).setAttributes(attrib);

    item = item.getNextSibling();
  };

  tgtBody.getChild(0).removeFromParent();
};
```

The following `include` helper function puts external JS/CSS contents from other files (filename given as argument) into the HTML file:

```
function include(filename) {
  return HtmlService.createHtmlOutputFromFile(filename)
    .getContent();
}
```

Create a new HTML file (`Sidebar.html`) from the **File** menu and enter the following code:

```
<!DOCTYPE html>
<html>
  <head>
    <base target="_top">
    <script src="//polymerstaticfiles.appspot.com/bower_components
    /webcomponentsjs/webcomponents.js"></script>

    <link rel="import"
    href="//polymerstaticfiles.appspot.com/bower_components
    /polymer/polymer.html">

    <link rel="import"
    href="//polymerstaticfiles.appspot.com/
    bower_components/font-roboto/roboto.html">

    <link rel="import"
    href="//polymerstaticfiles.appspot.com/
    bower_components/paper-input/paper-input.html">

    <link rel="import"
    href="//polymerstaticfiles.appspot.com/
    bower_components/paper-button/paper-button.html">

    <link rel="import"
    href="//polymerstaticfiles.appspot.com/
    bower_components/paper-checkbox/paper-checkbox.html">

    <link rel="import"
    href="//polymerstaticfiles.appspot.com/
    bower_components/paper-radio-group/paper-radio-group.html">

    <link rel="import"
    href="//polymerstaticfiles.appspot.com/
    bower_components/paper-radio-button/paper-radio-button.html">
```

```
    <link rel="import"
    href="//polymerstaticfiles.appspot.com/
    bower_components/paper-input/paper-input-decorator.html">

    <!-- Insert CSS code -->
    <?!= include('Sidebar.css.html'); ?>
  </head>

  <body>
    <div class="sidebar">
      <h4>Translate into</h4>
      <paper-radio-group id="dest">
        <paper-radio-button name="en" id="radio-dest-en"
        label="English"></paper-radio-button>

        <paper-radio-button name="fr" id="radio-dest-fr"
        label="French"></paper-radio-button>

        <paper-radio-button name="de" id="radio-dest-de"
        label="German"></paper-radio-button>

        <paper-radio-button name="ja" id="radio-dest-ja"
        label="Japanese"></paper-radio-button>

        <paper-radio-button name="es" id="radio-dest-es"
        label="Spanish"></paper-radio-button>
      </paper-radio-group>

      <br /><br />
      <hr />

      <paper-checkbox id="save-prefs" label="Use this
       language by default"></paper-checkbox>

      <div id="button-bar">
        <paper-button raised class="colored" id="run-
        translation">Translate</paper-button>
      </div>
    </div>

    <!-- Insert JS code -->
    <?!= include('Sidebar.js.html'); ?>
  </body>
</html>
```

In the preceding code, Google's polymer components library is used. Although we could have used simple HTML elements, we used polymer components for an aesthetic look and feel of the sidebar. You need not worry about the functioning of that library, you just need to include the URLs as shown. The `include` helper function inserts the respective file, given as argument, contents.

Create another HTML file and name it as `Sidebar.css`, including `.css`. The script editor will add `.html` extension, so the filename will be `Sidebar.css.html`. Enter the following code in it:

```
<style>
  body {
    font-family: 'RobotoDraft', sans-serif;
    margin: 0;
    padding: 0;
  }

  h4 {
    text-align: center;
    margin: 0;
  }

  paper-button {
    margin: 0;
    margin-top: 10px;
  }

  .sidebar {
    -moz-box-sizing: border-box;
    box-sizing: border-box;
    overflow-y: auto;
    padding: 12px;
    position: absolute;
    width: 100%;
  }

  #dest {
    margin-top: 5px;
  }

  .error {
    color: #dd4b39;
    font-size: small;
```

```
    margin-top: 8px;
  }

  .colored {
    background: #4285f4;
    color: #ffffff;
  }
</style>
```

The preceding CSS code defines styles for the HTML elements in the `Sidebar.html` file. CSS defines element styles within associated braces.

For example:

- The `body` style name defines styles for the body element
- `h4` defines styles for fourth-level heading elements
- The style name prefixed with a dot (`.`) defines styles for the elements, which belong to that class
- The name prefixed with the hash symbol (#) defines styles for element whose ID is same as the style name

 For further reading on CSS, refer to `https://developer.mozilla.org/en-US/Learn/CSS`.

Create another HTML file and name it `Sidebar.js`. Enter the following code in the newly created `Sidebar.js.html` file:

```
<script
src="//ajax.googleapis.com/ajax/libs/jquery/1.9.1/jquery.min.js"></
script>

<script>
  /**
    * On document load, assign click handlers to each button and
    * try to load the user's origin and destination language
    * preferences, if previously set.
    *
    */
  $(function() {
    $('#run-translation').click(runTranslation);

    google.script.run
      .withSuccessHandler(loadPreferences)
```

```
      .withFailureHandler(showError).getPreferences();
});


/**
 * Callback function that populates the origin and destination
 * selection boxes with user preferences from the server.
 *
 */
function loadPreferences(languagePrefs) {
  if (languagePrefs.destLang){
    $('#dest').prop('selected', languagePrefs.destLang);
  }
}


/**
 * Runs a server-side function to translate the text.
 *
 */
function runTranslation() {
  this.disabled = true;
  $('#error').remove();

  var dest = $('#dest').prop('selected');
  var savePrefs = $('#save-prefs').prop('checked');

  google.script.run
    .withSuccessHandler(
      function(msg, element) {
        element.disabled = false;
      })
    .withFailureHandler(
      function(msg, element) {
        showError(msg, $('#button-bar'));
        element.disabled = false;
      })
    .withUserObject(this)
    .runTranslation(dest, savePrefs);
}
```

```
/**
 * Inserts a div that contains an error message after a given
 * element.
 *
 */
function showError(msg, element) {
  var div = $('<div id="error" class="error">' + msg +
  '</div>');

  $(element).after(div);
}
</script>
```

After typing all the code without errors, reload the document. A new entry **Translate** under the **Add-ons** menu will appear. Click on **start** to open the sidebar, which will have all the controls you need to run the application. To test the application, enter some text in the source document (in which you have entered code). Select language into which you would like to translate the text, then click on the **TRANSLATE** button.

The translated text will be placed in the destination document whose ID you entered in the code. Open that document to see the translated text.

The following screenshot shows the sidebar:

The following screenshot shows the source document text in English before translation:

> After entering all the codes without error, reload the document. A new entry 'Translate' under Add-ons
>
> menu will appear. Click on start to open the sidebar, which will have all the controls you need to run the
>
> application. To test the application enter some text in the source document (in which you have entered
>
> code). Select language into which you would like to translate the text then click on TRANSLATE button.

Now if you open the target document, then you can view the translated text saved in it. The sample text shown in the preceding screenshot is translated to Japanese as shown here:

> エラーなしですべてのコードを入力した後、ドキュメントをリロードします。 Add-onsサイ
> トのメニューの下に新しいエントリ「翻訳」は表示されます。アプリケーションを実行する
> ために必要なすべてのコントロールを持つことになり、サイドバーを開くには、スタートを
> クリックします。アプリケーションをテストするには（あなたがコードを入力したした）元
> の文書にテキストを入力します。あなたが翻訳ボタンをクリックし、テキストを翻訳したい
> 先の言語を選択します。

Creating a document reviewing and instant inline commenting application

We will create a document reviewing and commenting application. The document can be an article submission, a comprehension submitted by a student, a thesis paper submitted by a researcher, or anything else that should be reviewed before acceptance. The reviewer can review and insert predefined comments or his/her own custom comments, instantly. The reviewer selects some text in the document, and clicks on any one button (predefined comments) to highlight. Then, the script will highlight the text and insert the comment text inline along with creating an actual comment. You can see the created comments in the **Comment** panel (at the top right-hand side). Finally, the reviewer can insert score at the end of the document.

As usual, create the `onOpen` trigger function in the code file, and it will open the sidebar:

```
function onOpen() {
  var ui = HtmlService.createHtmlOutputFromFile('Sidebar')
    .setTitle('Review and Comment');

  DocumentApp.getUi().showSidebar(ui);
}
```

The `insertComment` function inserts the actual comment into the document. Drive is an advanced service, so you should enable the Drive API before using it. I hope you remember how to enable advanced services. If you don't, then revise from *Chapter 5, Creating Google Calendar and Drive Applications*:

```
function insertComment(comment, selectedText){
  // You should enable this advanced service (Drive API).
  Drive.Comments.insert(
    {
      "content": comment,
      "context": {"type":"text/html", "value":selectedText},
    },
    DocumentApp.getActiveDocument().getId()
  );
}
```

The `insertText` function uses the selected text or the text where the cursor is pointed to as an argument:

```
/**
 * Replaces the text of the current selection with the provided
 * text, or inserts text at the current cursor location.
 * (There will always be either a selection or a cursor.)
 * If multiple elements are selected, only inserts the text in the
 * first element that can contain text.
 *
 * @param {string} newText The text with which to replace the
 *                 current selection.
 *
 */
function insertText(newText) {
  var selection = DocumentApp.getActiveDocument().getSelection();

  // If any text selected then get selected text else cursor.
  if (selection) {
```

```
  var elements = selection.getRangeElements();
  for (var i = 0; i < elements.length; i++) {
    var startIndex = elements[i].getStartOffset();
    var endIndex = elements[i].getEndOffsetInclusive();

    // If picture/image element selected.
    if(startIndex == endIndex) throw "Error: Select text only.";

    // Highlight the selected text.
    var element = elements[i].getElement()
        .setBackgroundColor(startIndex, endIndex, '#f6d2ab');

    // Insert selected comment next to the selected text.
    element.insertText(endIndex+1, '[' + newText +']')
        .setBackgroundColor(
          endIndex+1, endIndex+newText.length+2, '#bbffbb'
        );

    var text = element.getText()
        .substring(
          startIndex,endIndex+1
        );

    // Call insertComment function
    insertComment(newText,text);
  }

} else {

  var curr = DocumentApp.getActiveDocument().getCursor();

  // Exit if document not active or cursor not in document.
  if(!curr) return;

  // Insert comment and call insertComment function.
  curr.insertText('[' + newText +']')
    .setBackgroundColor('#bbffbb');

  insertComment(newText);
  }
}
```

This `insertScore` function inserts a horizontal line at the end of the document, and it also inserts the score based on whether the document meets the expectation or not:

```
function insertScore(newText){
  var doc = DocumentApp.getActiveDocument();
  var body = doc.getBody();

  body.appendHorizontalRule();
  body.appendParagraph(newText)
    .setAttributes({FONT_SIZE:24,FOREGROUND_COLOR:'#6aa84f'});
}
```

Create the following code in the `Sidebar.html` file:

```html
<!-- Sidebar.html -->
<!DOCTYPE html>
<html>
  <head>
    <base target="_top">

    <!-- Google's add-on stylesheet -->
    <link rel="stylesheet"
    href="https://ssl.gstatic.com/docs/script/css/add-ons1.css" />

    <!-- jQuery UI stylesheet -->
    <link rel="stylesheet"
    href="//ajax.googleapis.com/ajax/libs/jqueryui/
    1.10.4/themes/smoothness/jquery-ui.css" />

    <!-- jQuery base library -->
    <script
    src="//ajax.googleapis.com/ajax/libs/jquery/
    1.10.2/jquery.min.js"></script>

    <!-- jQuery UI library -->
    <script
    src="//ajax.googleapis.com/ajax/libs/
    jqueryui/1.10.2/jquery-ui.min.js"></script>

    <!-- Add additional styles -->
    <style>
      select{ height:35px; }

      textarea{
        width:100%;
```

```
      margin-top: 3px;
      margin-bottom: 3px;
    }

    .blue{
      -moz-border-radius: 3px;
      -webkit-border-radius: 3px;
      border-radius: 3px;
    }

    .blue + .blue{
      margin: .5px -.5px;
    }

    .ui-accordion .ui-accordion-header {
      display: block;
      cursor: pointer;
      position: relative;
      margin-top: 1px;
      padding: .4em .25em .4em .25em;
      min-height: 0; /* support: IE7 */
    }

    .ui-accordion .ui-accordion-icons {
      padding-left: 2em;
    }

    .ui-accordion .ui-accordion-content {
      padding: .5em .5em;
      overflow: auto;
    }
  </style>
</head>
```

The accordion block's structure is provided in the code comment:

```
<body>
  <!-- To comply with the jQuery UI library,
       The accordion should be in the form:
    <div id="accordion">
      <h3>Section 1</h3>
      <div>
         ...
      </div>
```

```
        <h3>Section 2</h3>
        <div>
          ...
        </div>
    </div>
-->

<div id="accordion">

    <h3>Comments</h3>
    <div>
        <b>Highlight text and click the appropriate comment</b>
        <div id="button-bar">
          <button class="blue comment-button"
            value = "Awkward">Awkward</button>

          <button class="blue comment-button"
            value = "Citation Needed">Citation Needed</button>

          <button class="blue comment-button"
            value="Improper Citation">Improper Citation</button>

          <button class="blue comment-button"
            value="Commonly Confused">Commonly Confused</button>

          <button class="blue comment-button"
            value="Delete">Delete</button>

          <button class="blue comment-button"
            value="Run-on">Run-on</button>

          <button class="blue comment-button"
            value="Vague">Vague</button>
        </div>

        <div>
          <textarea rows="3" id="insert-text"
            placeholder="Type your comment here"></textarea>
        </div>

        <div>
          <button class="blue" id="insert-button">Comment</button>
        </div>
    </div>
```

```
    <h3>Scores</h3>
    <div>
      <div id="score-bar">
        Does the document meet the expectation?
        <br />
        <button class="green insert-score" value="Meets"
          >Yes</button>

        <button class="green insert-score" value="Not Yet"
          >No</button>
      </div>
    </div>
</div>

<script>
  // On document load assign the events.
  $(function(){

    /**
     * Which accordion block should be active/expanded by
     * default, here the first one.
     *
     */
    $("#accordion").accordion({ active: 0 });

    // Assign a click event to buttons.
    $(".comment-button").click(insertButtonComment);
    $("#insert-button").click(insertCustomComment);
    $(".insert-score").click(insertScore);

  });


  /**
   *   Runs a server-side function to insert pre-defined
   *   comment into the document at the cursor
   *   or after the selection.
   *
   */
  function insertButtonComment() {
    this.disabled = true;
    $('#error').remove();
```

```
        google.script.run
          .withSuccessHandler(
            function(returnSuccess, element) {
              element.disabled = false;
            }
          )
          .withFailureHandler(
            function(msg, element) {
              showError(msg, $('#button-bar'));
              element.disabled = false;
            }
          )
          .withUserObject(this)
          .insertText($(this).val());
      }


      /**
       *  Runs a server-side function to insert custom comment
       *  into the document on pointing the cursor or
       *  after the selection.
       *
       */
      function insertCustomComment() {
        this.disabled = true;
        $('#error').remove();

        google.script.run
          .withSuccessHandler(
            function(returnSuccess, element) {
              element.disabled = false;
            }
          )
          .withFailureHandler(
            function(msg, element) {
              showError(msg, $('#button-bar'));
              element.disabled = false;
            }
          )
          .withUserObject(this)
          .insertText($('#insert-text').val());
      }
```

```
/**
 *  Runs a server-side function to insert the score
 *
 */
function insertScore() {
this.disabled = true;
$('#error').remove();

google.script.run
  .withSuccessHandler(
    function(returnSuccess, element) {
      element.disabled = false;
    }
  )
  .withFailureHandler(
    function(msg, element) {
      showError(msg, $('#score-bar'));
      element.disabled = false;
    }
  )
  .withUserObject(this)
  .insertScore($(this).val());
}

/**
 *  Inserts a div that contains an error message after a
 *  given element.
 *
 *  @param msg-The error message to display.
 *  @param element-The element after which to display the
 *                 error.
 *
 */
function showError(msg, element) {
  var div = $('<div id="error" class="error">'
      + msg + '</div>');

  $(element).after(div);
}
    </script>
  </body>
</html>
```

The following screenshot shows the sidebar and document:

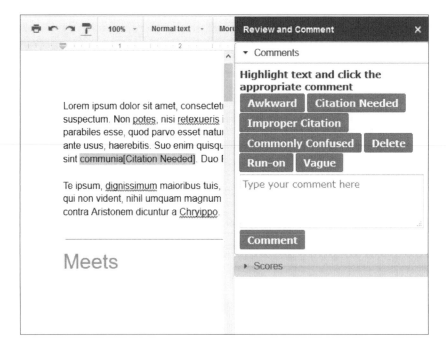

You can see the inserted comments by clicking on the **Comment** button at the top right-hand side corner of the document's window.

Summary

In this chapter, you learned and created many useful applications, including an RSS/Atom reader, the language translator applications, and the document reviewing and commenting application. In the next chapter, you will learn to create interactive web pages, an RSS feed, a file upload, and a timesheet application.

7

Creating Interactive Webpages

In the previous chapter, you learned to create an RSS/Atom feed reader, stock quote ticker, language translator, and to create a document reviewing and commenting application.

In this chapter, you will learn:

- To create web applications that return Sheet data as HTML, JSON, and PDF
- To send HTTP/HTTPS request with the query string
- To create an RSS feed
- To create a file upload application
- To create a timesheet application

Creating a web app to render Sheet data as HTML

We will create an application to return Sheet data as HTML in the browser. Create a Sheet, rename it as Data, and populate it with some test data as shown in the next screenshot. You can populate the Sheet with any random data with the three columns named First Name, Last Name, and Full Name:

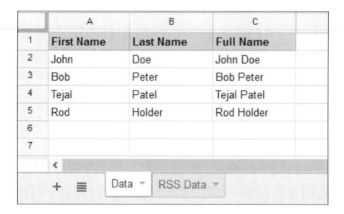

In the Code.gs file, create the doGet function as shown here:

```
function doGet() {
  /*
   *   This spreadsheet may not be active while this function
   *   executes, so you cannot get access to active spreadsheet,
   *   use open by id.
   *
   */
  var ss = SpreadsheetApp
      .openById("Replace with this spreadsheet id");

  var SheetData = ss.getSheetByName("Data");

  var data = SheetData.getDataRange().getValues();

  var html = '<!DOCTYPE html><html><body><table border=1>';

  // Each row data passed as argument to the anonymous function.
  data.forEach(function(row){
    html += '<tr>';
    html += '<td>' + row[0] + '</td>';
```

```
    html += '<td>' + row[1] + '</td>';
    html += '<td>' + row[2] + '</td>';
    html += '</tr>';
  });

  // Let's close table, body and html tags.
  html += '</table></body></html>';

  // Return as HTML document.
  Return HtmlService.createHtmlOutput(html);


}
```

The `HtmlService` function can be used to create any HTML content. The preceding `doGet` function returns HTML content created by `HtmlService` to the browser. Publish the script as explained earlier, and enter the URL in the browser's address bar. You can see the result as shown in the following screenshot. The data shown may vary as per your input data.

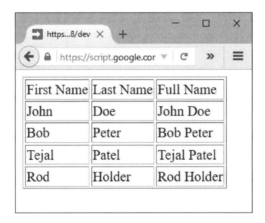

Creating a web app to return JSON

Now, we will see how to return JSON string instead of HTML content. In the `Data` Sheet, add another column named DOB as shown here:

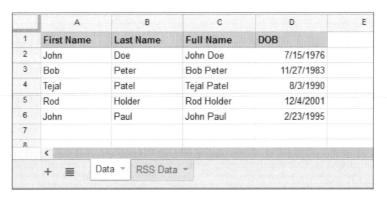

Create the `doGet` function as shown here:

```
function doGet(){
  /*
   *   This spreadsheet may not be active while this function
   *   executes, so you cannot get access to active spreadsheet,
   *   use open by id.
   *
   */
  var ss = SpreadsheetApp
      .openById("Replace with this spreadsheet id");

  var SheetData = ss.getSheetByName("Data");

  var data = SheetData.getDataRange().getValues();

  // Remove header
  data.shift();

  var date = new Date();
  var currYear = date.getFullYear();

  var output = {};

  data.forEach(function(row){
    var dob = new Date(row[3]);
    var dobYear = dob.getFullYear();
```

```
    /*
     * Create full name property within output object.
     * Again the full name property is an object.
     *
     */
    output[row[2]] = {};

    /*
     * Assign DOB property to full name object.
     * Change time zone and date format as per your preference.
     *
     */
    output[row[2]].dob = Utilities
      .formatDate(row[3], "UTC", "MM/dd/yyyy");

    // Let's calculate age.
    output[row[2]].age = currYear - dobYear;
  });

  // We can return only string to browser, so convert to string.
  var json = JSON.stringify(output);

  return ContentService.createTextOutput(json);
}
```

The output in the browser will be JSON string as follows:

Converting Sheet data as a PDF file

You can create an application to convert Sheet data into a PDF file and store it in Drive, and return the PDF file's URL to the user:

In the `Code.gs` file, create the `doGet` function as listed here:

```
function doGet() {
  /*
   *  This spreadsheet may not be active while this function
   *  executes, so you cannot get access to active spreadsheet,
   *  use open by id.
   *
   */
  var ss = SpreadsheetApp.openById("[[ this spreadsheet id ]]");

  var SheetData = ss.getSheetByName("Data");

  var template = HtmlService
      .createTemplateFromFile("Template.html");

  // Assign 'data' to the template object
  template.data = SheetData.getDataRange().getValues();

  // Evaluate template object as html content
  var html = template.evaluate();

  // Convert html content to pdf
  // var pdf = html.getAs("application/pdf")
  //    .setName("Test_Data.pdf");

  // Or use this code
  var pdf = html.getAs(MimeType.PDF).setName("Test_Data.pdf");

  // Create pdf file in the "My Drive" folder and share it with
  //public.
  var file = DriveApp.createFile(pdf);

  // Let's set sharing access as anyone can view the pdf.
  file.setSharing(
    DriveApp.Access.ANYONE_WITH_LINK, DriveApp.Permission.VIEW
  );
```

```
    // Create and return html content with link to the pdf file.
    return HtmlService.createHtmlOutput(
      'Click <a target="_top" href="'
      + file.getUrl()
      +'">here</a> to view pdf file.'
    );
  }
```

Create a new HTML file, `Template.html`, and enter the following HTML code. In this code, the `data` array is a 2-dimensional array already assigned to the `template` object in the `doGet` function:

```
<!DOCTYPE html>
<html>
  <body>
    <table>
      <? for(var i in data) {?>
        <tr>
          <? for(var j in data[i]) { ?>
            <td><?= data[i][j] ?></td>
          <? } ?>
        </tr>
      <? } ?>
    </table>
  </body>
</html>
```

In the mentioned code, the template markers `<?` and `?>` enclose the script code, which is identical to the `script` tag in the normal HTML code. The enclosed code executes, but does not return anything. The markers `<?=` and `?>` return the result of the enclosed code. For example, `<?= data[i][j] ?>` returns the *i*th row *j*th column value of a 2-dimensional `data` array.

For your understanding the server script without template markup in the previous code is reproduced here:

```
for(var i in data) {
  for(var j in data[i]) {
    data[i][j]
  }
}
```

Publish and enter the published URL in a browser's address bar. The result will be as shown in the following screenshot. Click on the hyperlink to open the PDF file in Drive:

A sample output of the created PDF as per the Sheet data is shown in the following screenshot. The output may vary as per your input data:

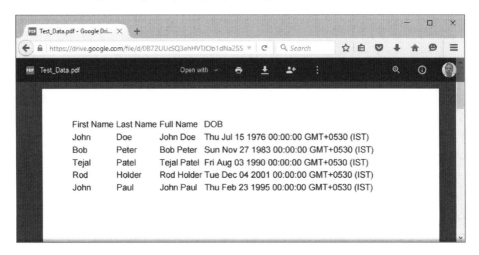

Sending an HTTP/HTTPS request with query string

You can send an HTTP/HTTPS request along with the query string. To do this, append the published URL with your query string.

For example: `https://script.google.com/macros/s/AKfycbxa4ErKHiX_0gQ0JUU-Q1qMhvRrOsrx3HXuVZp7pzX8UVxMu4w/exec?`**`fname=John`**

```
function doGet(e){
  Logger.log(e);
}
```

A sample of the logged HTTP/HTTPS request's event object is shown here:

```
Logs

[15-12-06 03:51:40:240 IST] {parameter={fname=John}, contextPath=, contentLength=-1,
queryString=fname=John, parameters={fname=[John]}}
```

The doGet function listed in the following code snippet shows how you can use the event object to get the required parameters for further processing:

```javascript
function doGet(e){

    // Get the fname value from the query string.
    var firstName = e.parameter.fname;

    /*
     *   There is no active spreadsheet, so you should open by id.
     *   Use the id of the spreadsheet in which your script resides.
     *
     */
    var ss = SpreadsheetApp.openById("Replace spreadsheet id");

    var SheetData = ss.getSheetByName("Data");

    var data = SheetData.getDataRange().getValues();

    // Remove header
    data.shift();

    var date = new Date();

    // Let's get the year in 4 digits.
    var currYear = date.getFullYear();

    var output = {};

    // Let's populate output with dob and age properties.
    data.forEach(function(row){
```

```
    // Skip if first name not match.
    if(firstName !== row[0]) return;

    var dob = new Date(row[3]);
    var dobYear = dob.getFullYear();

    output[row[2]] = {};
    output[row[2]].dob = Utilities
       .formatDate(row[3], "UTC", "MM/dd/yyyy");

    output[row[2]].age = currYear - dobYear;
  });

  var json = JSON.stringify(output);

  return ContentService.createTextOutput(json);
}
```

The mentioned doGet function gets the fname parameter from the query string and returns the calculated age value along with dob for matching fname.

Creating RSS feed using ContentService

You created an RSS reader application in *Chapter 6, Creating Feed Reader and Translator Applications*. Now, you can create an application to publish an RSS feed. Put the RSS data in a Sheet as shown here:

	A	B	C	D
1	**Title**	**Url**	**Author**	
2	Item 1 title	www.example.com	Author name 1	
3	Item 2 title	Link to the item 2	Author name 2	
4	Item 3 title	Link to the item 3	Author name 3	
5	Item 4 title	Link to the item 4	Author name 4	
6	Item 5 title	Link to the item 5	Author name 5	
7				
8				

RSS Data ▾

Also, edit/enter the following doGet function:

```
function doGet() {
  /*
   *   There is no active spreadsheet, so you should open by id.
   *   Use the id of the spreadsheet in which your script resides.
   *
   */
  var ss = SpreadsheetApp.openById([[ this spreadsheet id ]]);

  var SheetRss = ss.getSheetByName("RSS Data");

  var rssData = SheetRss.getDataRange().getValues();

  // Remove header.
  rssData.shift();

  var strRss = '<?xml version="1.0" encoding="UTF-8"?>';

  // Root element.
  strRss += '<rss>';

  // Open channel element.
  strRss += '<channel>';

  // Add description and language elements.
  strRss += '<description>A brief description of the
  channel</description>';
  strRss += '<language>en-US</language>';
```

```
    // Each row data is passed as an argument to the anonymous
    //function.
    rssData.forEach(function(row){
      strRss += '<item>';
      strRss += '<title>' + row[0] + '</title>';
      strRss += '<link>' + row[1] + '</link>';
      strRss += '<creator>' + row[2] + '</creator>';
      strRss += '</item>';
    });

    // Close channel and root (rss) elements.
    strRss += '</channel></rss>';

    // Return as RSS xml document.
    return ContentService
      .createTextOutput(strRss)
      .setMimeType(ContentService.MimeType.RSS);
  }
```

Publish the script as you did before. You can use the published URL as the RSS URL in your RSS reader application built in the previous chapter.

Creating a file upload application

You can create an application to upload any file to Drive from the browser. Create the doGet and uploadFiles functions in the Code.gs file as listed here:

In the Code.gs file, add this code:

```
function doGet() {
  // Let's return html page created from the Form.html file.
  return HtmlService.createHtmlOutputFromFile('Form.html')
    .setTitle("File Upload");
};

function uploadFiles(form) {
  // You can change the folder name as you like.
  var folderName = "Uploaded Files";

  var folder, folders = DriveApp.getFoldersByName(folderName);

  // folders is an iterator.
  if (folders.hasNext()) folder = folders.next();
```

```
    // Let's create a folder if it does not exist.
    else folder = DriveApp.createFolder(folderName);

    // Let's create the file, got from the form, within the folder.
    var file = folder.createFile(form.file);

    // Let's return the file's url
    return file.getUrl();
}
```

The `uploadFiles` function looks for an existing folder with the name `Uploaded Files`. If not found, then it creates the same within root, `My Drive`, folder. Subsequently, it creates the file passed with the argument and returns the created file's URL.

Update the code in the `Form.html` file:

```html
<!DOCTYPE html>
<html>
  <head>
    <base target="_top">

    <link rel="stylesheet"
     href="//ssl.gstatic.com/docs/script/css/add-ons1.css"/>
    <script
     src="//ajax.googleapis.com/ajax/libs/jquery
     /1.10.2/jquery.min.js"></script>
  </head>

  <body>
    <div class="sidebar">
      <form>
        <input type="file" name="file">
        <br /><br />
        <input type="button" id="upload"
          class="submit" value="Upload">
      </form>
    </div>

    <script>
      $(function(){
        $("#upload").click(fileUpload);
      });
```

```
function fileUpload(){
  this.disabled = true;
  google.script.run
    .withSuccessHandler(function(msg, element){
      element.disabled = false;
      showSucces(msg);
    })
    .withFailureHandler(function(msg, element) {
      element.disabled = false;
      showError(msg, element);
    })
    .withUserObject(this)
    .uploadFiles(this.parentNode);
}

function showSucces(msg) {
  alert("File uploaded successfully.
    \n The file url is: " + msg);
}

function showError(msg, element) {
  var div = $('<div id="error" class="error">'
    + msg + '</div>');

  $(element).after(div);
}


    </script>
  </body>
</html>
```

The preceding code renders the upload form controls, and if **Upload** is clicked, then it calls the `uploadFiles` server function.

A sample of the file upload form's controls is shown here:

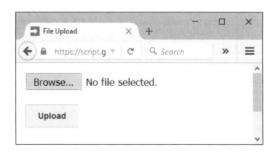

Click on the **Browse...** button to select any file stored locally. Then, click on the **Upload** button to upload to Drive. The selected file will be uploaded to the `Uploaded Files` folder within the `My Drive` folder.

After a successful upload, an alert box with the uploaded file's URL will be displayed as shown in the following screenshot. You can use the URL to verify the successful file upload.

Creating an employee timesheet application

From the knowledge and experience gathered by creating the preceding applications, you can create this full blown timesheet application. This application can be used in an organization or company to log employees, worked hours in a day or shift. The daily attendance data will be backed in the `Backup` Sheet for future reference.

Create a new spreadsheet with a Sheet named `EmployeesList` and populate it with employee names. All these names will be listed as a dropdown automatically in the user interface.

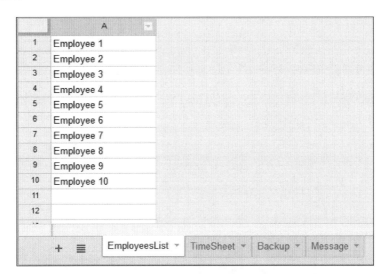

Create another Sheet named `TimeSheet` and arrange the column headers as shown in the following screenshot. Ensure columns *C*, *D*, *E*, and *F* are formatted as `date`, otherwise date may be shown as epoch number. Leave column *A* blank as it will be used by the script to mark the status of a shift such as `sb` (shift begin), `bb` (break begin), `be` (break end), and `se` (shift end).

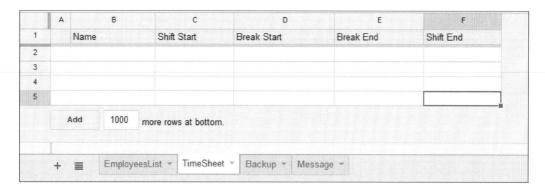

Create another Sheet with the name `Backup`, which is used to back up every day's shift data from the `TimeSheet` Sheet. Arrange the columns as shown here. Remember to format columns *B*, *C*, *D*, and *E* as `date`.

Create another new Sheet and name it as `Message`, which will be used to pass a message, if any, to employees:

In the `Code.gs` file, create the global variables as well as the `doGet` and `getEmpNames` functions. Replace `[[ this spreadsheet id ]]` with the actual ID/key (as a string) of the spreadsheet in which you are editing the code:

```
var ssid = "[[ this spreadsheet id ]]";

// Change date format as per your preference.
var DF = "MM/dd/yyyy HH:mm:ss";
var TZ = Session.getScriptTimeZone();

var ss = SpreadsheetApp.openById(ssid);
var TimeSheet = ss.getSheetByName("TimeSheet");
var EmpSheet = ss.getSheetByName("EmployeesList");
var BackupSheet = ss.getSheetByName("Backup");
var MessageSheet = ss.getSheetByName("Message");
```

This `getEmpList` function creates and returns employee names as an array:

```
/**
 *  Get employee names from the EmployeesList sheet,
 *  construct the data as an array and return.
 *
 */
function getEmpList(){
  var emp = [];
  var data = EmpSheet.getDataRange().getValues();

  for(var i in data) if(data[i][0]) emp.push(data[i][0]);

  return emp;
}
```

In the `doGet` function, the message and employee list are assigned to the `template` object and returns evaluated HTML content:

```
function doGet(){
  var template = HtmlService.createTemplateFromFile("Timesheet");
  template.message = MessageSheet.getRange("A2").getValue();
  template.empList = getEmpList();

  var html = template.evaluate();
  return html;
}
```

This `getEmpStatus` function returns employee shift status as an array:

```
// Returns employee shift status as an array [status, name].
function getEmpStatus(emp){
  var empData = EmpSheet.getDataRange().getValues();
  var timeData = TimeSheet.getDataRange().getValues();

  // Remove header
  timeData.shift();

  for(var i in timeData){
    if(timeData[i][1] == emp)
      return [timeData[i][0],empData[j][1]];
  }

  // Return null if employee not in shift
  return ["",""];
}
```

The `fmtDate_` function is a helper function that returns the formatted date string:

```
function fmtDate_(d, format){
  // Set the default date format, if 'format' not passed.
  var fmt = format || DF;

  return Utilities.formatDate(d, TZ, fmt);
}
```

The `postTime` function populates timesheet with respect to the employee name and what button he/she has clicked and these values are supplied as an argument (`name` and `val`). This function also throws errors, if any.

 The keyword throw returns an error object and terminates the execution.

```
function postTime(name, val){
  var time = fmtDate_(new Date());
  var data = TimeSheet.getDataRange().getValues();

  // If 'shift start' clicked
  if(val == "sb"){
    // Update start time if clicked again.
    for(var i in data){
      if(data[i][1] == name && data[i][0] == "sb" ){
```

```
      data[i][2] = time;
      TimeSheet.getRange(1, 1, data.length, data[0].length)
        .setValues(data);
      return [val,name];
    }
  };

  // Else insert new name and update start time.
  TimeSheet.appendRow([val,name,time]);

  return [val,name];
}

// If 'break start' clicked.
if(val == "bb"){
  for(var i in data){
    // Update break start time only if employee is in shift.
    if(data[i][0] == "sb" && data[i][1] == name ){
      data[i][0] = val;
      data[i][3] = time;

      TimeSheet.getRange(1, 1, data.length, data[0].length)
        .setValues(data);

      return [val,name];
    }
  };

  // If 'break start' clicked before 'shift start'.
  throw "Please start your shift.";
}

// If 'break end' clicked
if(val == "be"){
  for(var i in data){
    if(data[i][0] == "bb" && data[i][1] == name ){
      data[i][0] = val;
      data[i][4] = time;
      TimeSheet.getRange(1, 1, data.length, data[0].length)
        .setValues(data);
      return [val,name];
    }
  };
```

```
    // If 'break end' clicked before 'break start'.
    throw "Please start your break.";
  }


  // If shift end clicked
  if(val == "se"){
    for(var i in data){
      if(data[i][1] == name
          && (data[i][0] == "sb"|| data[i][0] == "be") ){
        var backup = [];
        backup.push(
          data[i][1],    // Name
          data[i][2],    // Shift Start
          data[i][3],    // Break Start
          data[i][4],    // Break End
          time,          // Shift end
          '=(E2-B2)*24', // Col F formula,
          '=(D2-C2)*24', // Col G formula
          '=F2-G2'       // Col H formula
        );


        /*
         * Copy Timesheet data to Backup sheet.
         * Insert a new row before row 2,
         * so that the inserted formulas ever work.
         *
         */
        BackupSheet.insertRowBefore(2);

        BackupSheet.getRange(2, 1, 1, backup.length)
          .setValues([backup]);

        /*
         * Tidy timesheet.
         * Ensure at least one data row before deleting,
         *  to avoid error.
         *
         */
        if(i<2) TimeSheet.appendRow(['']);

        // Delete copied row
        TimeSheet.deleteRow(Number(i)+1);
```

```
        return [val,name];
      }
    };

    // If 'shift end' clicked before 'break end'.
    if(data[i][0] == "bb")
      throw "Please end your break.";

    // If 'shift end' clicked without starting shift.
    throw "Please start your shift.";
    }
  }
}
```

The preceding postTime function populates data to the TimeSheet Sheet as per the button clicked by the user. Also, it throws errors if there are any conflicts in the shift time. For example, a user cannot click on **Break End** before **Break Start** and cannot click on **Shift Start** without ending the previous shift, and so on.

Create a new HTML file named as Timesheet and enter the following code in it:

```
<!DOCTYPE html>
<html>
  <head>
    <base target="_top">
    <link rel="stylesheet"
    href="https://ssl.gstatic.com/docs/script/css/add-ons.css" />
    <script
      src="https://ajax.googleapis.com/ajax/libs
      /jquery/1.10.1/jquery.min.js"></script>
  </head>

  <body>
    <div>
      <fieldset style="padding-bottom:25px;">
        <legend>Timesheet</legend>
        <select id="employee" name="employee">
          <? for(var i in empList){ ?>
              <option value="<?= empList[i] ?>" >
              <?= empList[i] ?></option>
          <? } ?>
        </select>
        <br /><br />
        <button id="sb" value="sb"><span>Shift
        Start</span></button>
```

```
      <button id="bb" value="bb"><span>Break
      Start</span></button>

      <button id="be" value="be"><span>Break End</span></button>
      <button id="se" value="se"><span>Shift End</span></button>
   </fieldset>

   <fieldset>
     <div id="message"><?!= message ?></div>
   </fieldset>
</div>

<script>
   $(function() {
     // Disable all buttons.
     $('#sb,#bb,#be,#se').prop("disabled", true);

     // Set drop-down change event.
     $('#employee').change(getStatus);

     // Set buttons click event.
     $('#sb,#bb,#be,#se').click(postTime);

     getStatus();
   });

   function getStatus(){
     // Remove all previous error messages.
     $('#error,#success').remove();

     // Disable all buttons.
     $('#sb,#bb,#be,#se').prop("disabled", true);

     // Get employee shift status.
     google.script.run
       .withSuccessHandler(function(status){
         updateStatus(status);
       })
       .getEmpStatus($("#employee").val());
   }

   function postTime(){
     // Remove all previous error messages.
```

```
        $('#error,#success').remove();

        // Disable all buttons.
        $('#sb,#bb,#be,#se').prop("disabled", true);

        // Post shift time to sheet.
        google.script.run
          .withSuccessHandler(function(msg){
            updateStatus(msg[0]);
          })
          .withFailureHandler(function(msg, elm){
            showError(msg, elm);
          })
          .withUserObject(this)
          .postTime($("#employee").val(),$(this).val());
      }


      function updateStatus(status){
        // Enable appropriate buttons only.
        switch(status){
          case "sb": $('#bb,#se').prop("disabled", false); break;
          case "bb": $('#be').prop("disabled", false); break;
          case "be": $('#se').prop("disabled", false); break;
          default: $('#sb').prop("disabled", false);
        }
      }


      function showError(msg, elm) {
        var span = $('<span id="error" class="error">'
        + msg + '</span>');
        $(elm).after(span);
      }

    </script>
  </body>
</html>
```

Publish the script and enter the published URL in the browser's address bar, then you will get the timesheet application loaded as shown in the screenshot. Experiment by selecting employee names from the dropdown and by clicking on buttons next to it. For every user action, the Timesheet and/or Backup Sheet data will be updated.

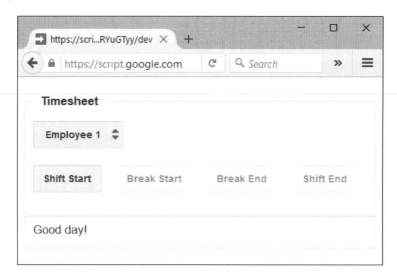

A sample output of the Timesheet data is shown here:

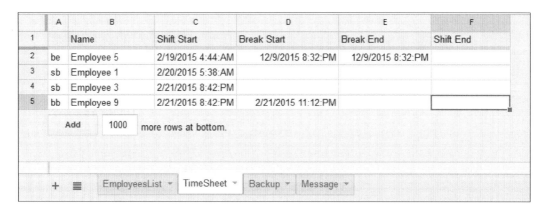

	A	B	C	D	E	F
1		Name	Shift Start	Break Start	Break End	Shift End
2	be	Employee 5	2/19/2015 4:44:AM	12/9/2015 8:32:PM	12/9/2015 8:32:PM	
3	sb	Employee 1	2/20/2015 5:38:AM			
4	sb	Employee 3	2/21/2015 8:42:PM			
5	bb	Employee 9	2/21/2015 8:42:PM	2/21/2015 11:12:PM		

Add 1000 more rows at bottom.

+ ≡ EmployeesList ▾ TimeSheet ▾ Backup ▾ Message ▾

As soon as the user clicks on **Shift End**, then the corresponding data from the TimeSheet Sheet will be transferred to the Backup Sheet and formulas will be created for the Shift Hours, Break Time, and Worked Hours columns. These formulas calculate the date difference and multiply it by 24 to show it as an hour value. A sample output of the Backup Sheet is shown here:

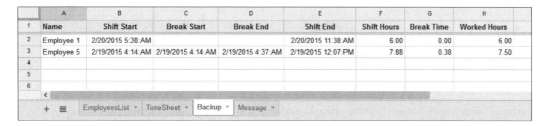

Summary

In this chapter, you learned and created many useful real-life applications including RSS publisher and a full-blown timesheet application. In the next chapter, you will create an order processing workflow application.

8
Building a Workflow Application

In the previous chapter, you learned to create interactive web pages using `ContentService`, `HtmlService`, `doGet`, and `doPost` functions. You also built RSS feed and timesheet applications.

In this chapter, you will learn:

- To create a workflow application
- The workflow involved in an order processing system

A Google Sheet holds all data, needed to create a workflow application, on various steps. It acts as the backbone of the order processing system.

> While working on published web applications, keep in mind that the following script code versions are independent of each other:
>
> - The already saved versions
> - The published version
> - The last saved codes
>
> So remember to publish the App every time you make updates to the code.

Order processing workflow – steps explained

The following are the steps involved in the order processing workflow:

1. The user opens an online form and sends an order by mentioning the item, quantity, delivery address, and mode of payment.

2. The Google Sheet sends a confirmation e-mail to both the **User** and **Accounts** section.

3. The **Accounts** section verifies the payment and forwards it to the **Order Processing** section.

4. The **Order Processing** section dispatches the order to the delivery address and updates shipment details.

5. The user confirms the delivery.

You can also refer to the pictorial representation of these steps in the following image:

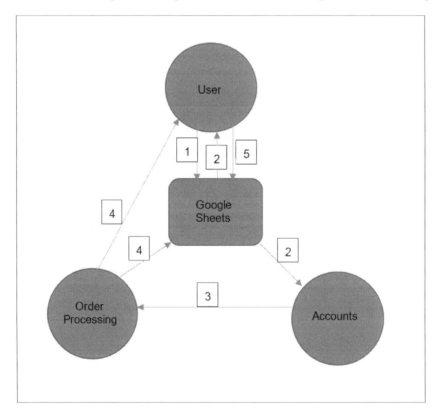

Configuring Google Sheets

Various forms, e-mails, and their components are explained here:

- User form:
    - Item
    - Unit price
    - Quantity
    - Total price (calculated)
    - Delivery address
    - Phone
    - E-mail
    - Payment details

 Upon the order submission, the script sends confirmation e-mails to both the **User** and **Accounts** section.

- Confirmation e-mail to the user:
    - Order number
    - Item
    - Unit price
    - Quantity
    - Total price
    - Delivery address
    - Phone number
    - Payment details

- E-mail to the **Accounts** section:

  It is same as the user confirmation e-mail; however, an additional link to the dispatch form is included.

 On receiving order e-mails, the **Accounts** section verifies if the payment details are okay, and then forwards that e-mail to the **Order Processing** section. The **Order Processing/ Dispatch** section clicks on the link to open the dispatch form, fills in shipment details, and submits the form.

- The dispatch form:
    - ○ Order number
    - ○ Item
    - ○ Quantity
    - ○ Delivery address
    - ○ Shipment details

 On the dispatch form submission, the script updates shipment details in the spreadsheet and sends a dispatch notification e-mail to the user.

- Post-dispatch e-mail to the user:
    - ○ Order number
    - ○ Delivery address
    - ○ Shipment details
    - ○ Acknowledge the delivery (link)

 The user clicks on the acknowledgement link, and then the script updates the delivery date corresponding to the order number row in the spreadsheet.

Now, create a new Google Sheet with two Sheets/tabs named Orders and Stock. Format the Orders Sheet column headers as shown in the following screenshot:

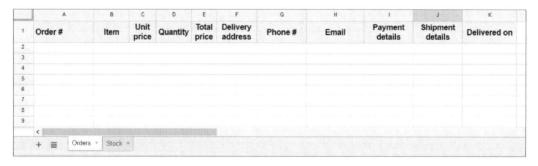

Format the `Stock` Sheet columns and populate the test data in it as shown here:

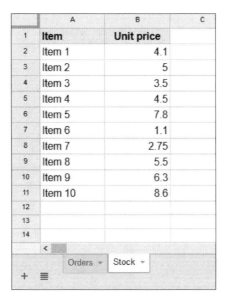

The items and corresponding unit prices will be populated in the `Orders` form.

Creating the Order form

In the `Code.gs` file, define the following global variables:

```
// Replace with your spreadsheet's ID.
var ss = SpreadsheetApp
    .openById("spreadsheet's id");

var SheetOrders = ss.getSheetByName("Orders");
var SheetStock = ss.getSheetByName("Stock");
```

Create the `doGet` function:

```
function doGet(){
   var template = HtmlService.createTemplateFromFile("Order");
   var html = template.evaluate();
   return HtmlService.createHtmlOutput(html);
}
```

The preceding function returns the `Order` form from the `Order.html` template. Create a new HTML file named `Order` and enter the following code in it:

```html
<!-- Order.html -->
<!DOCTYPE html>
<html>

  <head>
    <base target="_top">
  </head>

  <body>
    <form>
      <table>
        <tr>
        <td><label>Select Item:</label></td>
        <td>
          <select>
            <option value="Item 1">Item 1</option>
            <option value="Item 2">Item 2</option>
            <option value="Item 3">Item 3</option>
            <option value="Item 4">Item 4</option>
            <option value="Item 5">Item 5</option>
          </select>
        </td>
        </tr>

        <tr>
        <td><label>Unit price:</label></td>
        <td><input type="text" /></td>
        </tr>

        <tr>
        <td><label>Quantity:</label></td>
        <td><input type="number" value="1" /></td>
        </tr>

        <tr>
        <td><label>Total price:</label></td>
        <td><input type="text" /></td>
        </tr>
```

```
<tr>
<td><label>Deliver to:</label></td>
<td><textarea placeholder="Enter delivery address.">
</textarea></td>
</tr>

<tr>
<td><label>Phone:</label></td>
<td><input placeholder="Enter phone number." /></td>
</tr>

<tr>
<td><label>E-Mail:</label></td>
<td><input placeholder="Enter email address." /></td>
</tr>

<tr>
<td><label>Payment details:</label></td>
<td><input type="text"
        placeholder="Enter payment details." /></td>
</tr>
</table>

<br />
<input type="button" value="Submit" />
</form>
</body>

</html>
```

Publish the script using the following settings:

- Execute the app as:

  Me (your e-mail ID)

- Who has access to the app:

  Anyone, even anonymous

Click on the **Deploy** button, authorize if asked. The rendered application will be similar to the following screenshot:

This form is a basic one and not fancy. The item's selections are hard coded; only five fixed items. The user may not know the items which are currently available with the supplier, any new items that have been added to the list, or the current unit price for each item. Above all, we did not add any functionality to the **Submit** button.

Enhancing the Order form

To enhance the Order form, update the doGet function as follows:

```
function doGet(){
    var template = HtmlService.createTemplateFromFile("Order");
    template.pricelist = getPrice();

    var html = template.evaluate();
    return HtmlService.createHtmlOutput(html);
}
```

The price list is assigned to the template as a 2-dimensional array and is returned by the function shown here:

```
function getPrice(){
    var data = SheetStock.getDataRange().getValues();

    // remove header row.
    data.shift();

    return data;
}
```

In the `Order.html` file, update the `select` tag markup as shown in this code snippet:

```
<td>
    <select id="item" name="item">
        <? for(var i in pricelist){ ?>
            <option value="<?= pricelist[i][0] ?>" >
            <?= pricelist[i][0] ?></option>
        <? } ?>
    </select>
</td>
```

The drop-down items will reflect whatever is included or updated in the `Stock` Sheet. The default item will be the top-most or the first item in the list. So we have to put a default unit price for that item. Hence, update the **Unit price** input field as shown here:

```
<td><input id="unit_price" name="unit_price"
type="text" readonly value="<?= pricelist[0][1] ?>" /></td>
```

The `Order` form users are not going to enter the unit price, so it can be read only. We set default value for `quantity` as 1 and the default value for the total price as the unit price.

Update the `body` tag as follows:

```
<body>
    <form>
        <table>
            <tr>
            <td><label>Select Item:</label></td>
            <td><select id="item" name="item">
                <? for(var i in pricelist){ ?>
                    <option value="<?= pricelist[i][0] ?>" ><?=
                    pricelist[i][0] ?></option>
                <? } ?>
```

```
</select></td>
</tr>

<tr>
<td><label>Unit price:</label></td>
<td><input id="unit_price" name="unit_price" type="text"
     readonly value="<?= pricelist[0][1] ?>" /></td>
</tr>

<tr>
<td><label>Quantity:</label></td>
<td><input id="quantity" name="quantity" type="number"
     value="1" /></td>
</tr>

<tr>
<td><label>Total price:</label></td>
<td><input id="total_price" name="total_price" type="text"
     readonly value="<?= pricelist[0][1] ?>" /></td>
</tr>

<tr>
<td><label>Deliver to:</label></td>
<td><textarea name="delivery_address"
     placeholder="Enter delivery address.">
     </textarea></td>
</tr>

<tr>
<td><label>Phone:</label></td>
<td><input name="phone" type="phone"
     placeholder="Enter phone number." /></td>
</tr>

<tr>
<td><label>E-Mail:</label></td>
<td><input name="email" type="email"
     placeholder="Enter email address." /></td>
</tr>

<tr>
<td><label>Payment details:</label></td>
<td><input name="payment_details" type="text"
     placeholder="Enter payment details." /></td>
```

```
      </tr>
    </table>

    <br />
    <input class="blue" id="btnSubmit" type="button"
      value="Submit" />
  </form>
</body>
```

For the `select` element, we need an `onchange` event handler so that, if the user selects any item, the corresponding unit price should be retrieved from the spreadsheet and displayed in the **Unit price** input field. At the same time, the total price should be calculated as per quantity and unit price. Add script handlers along with the CSS style sheet in the `head` element. Update the code for the `head` tag as shown here:

```
<head>
  <base target="_top">

  <link rel="stylesheet"
   href="//ssl.gstatic.com/docs/script/css/add-ons1.css" />

  <script src="//ajax.googleapis.com/ajax/libs/
   jquery/1.10.2/jquery.min.js"></script>

  <script>
      // On document load, assigns events to elements.
      $(function(){
      $("#item").change(getUnitPrice);
      $("#quantity").change(calcTotalPrice);
      $("#btnSubmit").click(submit);
    });

    /*
     * Retrieves corresponding unit price for the selected item
     * and calculates the total price.
     *
     */
    function getUnitPrice(){
      google.script.run
      .withSuccessHandler(function(price){
        $("#unit_price").val(price);
        calcTotalPrice();
      })
```

```
          .getPrice( $("#item").prop("selectedIndex") );
      };

      function calcTotalPrice(){
        $("#total_price").val( $("#unit_price").val() *
        $("#quantity").val() );
      };

      function submit(){
        // Remove already displayed messages, if any.
        $("#success,#error").remove();

        this.disabled = true;

        google.script.run
          .withSuccessHandler(function(msg,elm){
            elm.disabled = false;
            showSuccess(msg,elm);
          })
          .withFailureHandler(function(msg, elm){
            elm.disabled = false;
            showError(msg, elm);
          })
          .withUserObject(this)
          .postOrder( this.parentNode );
          // submit button's parent, i.e. form.
      }


      function showSuccess(msg,elm) {
        var span = $('<span id="success">
        <font color="green"> ' + msg + '</font></span>');

        $(elm).after(span);
      }


      function showError(msg,elm) {
        var span = $('<span id="error" class="error"> '
        + msg + '</span>');

        $(elm).after(span);
      }
    </script>
  </head>
```

The `getPrice` server function needs to recognize the selected item index as an argument, so we will update it as shown here:

```
function getPrice(index){
    var data = SheetStock.getDataRange().getValues();

    // remove header row.
    data.shift();

    return typeof index == "undefined" ? data : data[index][1];
}
```

Now, this function works when called from the `doGet` function as well as from the preceding HTML client code. When called from the `doGet` function, it returns the complete price list, otherwise just the unit price of a selected item.

This helper function validates an e-mail. Returns `true` if valid otherwise `false`:

```
function isValidEmail_(email) {
    var regex = /^([\w-\.]+@([\w-]+\.)+[\w-]{2,6})?$/;
    return regex.test(email);
}
```

Next, add a form submission handler function (`postOrder`). If the order is placed, then this handler should update the spreadsheet and send an e-mail confirmation to the user as well as to the **Accounts** department:

```
function postOrder(form){

    // Validate user email
    if( !isValidEmail_(form.email) )
        throw "please provide a valid email id.";

    /*
     *   Date used as order number,
     *   which helps to have distinctive number.
     *   However, you may use any other number or string.
     *
     *   Prepend 'new' with '+' to get 'value' (number) of the date.
     *
     */
    var orderNumber = +new Date();

    // Construct form element values in an array.
    var order = [
        orderNumber,
        form.item,
```

```
      form.unit_price,
      form.quantity,
      form.total_price,
      form.delivery_address,
      form.phone,
      form.email,
      form.payment_details
];

SheetOrders.appendRow(order);

var htmlBody = "<p>Order number: " + orderNumber + "</p>";
htmlBody += "<p>Item: " + form.item + "</p>";
htmlBody += "<p>Unit price: " + form.unit_price + "</p>";
htmlBody += "<p>Quantity: " + form.quantity + "</p>";
htmlBody += "<p>Total price: " + form.total_price + "</p>";
htmlBody += "<p>Delivery address: " + form.delivery_address
            + "</p>";

htmlBody += "<p>Phone number: " + form.phone + "</p>";
htmlBody += "<p>Payment details: " + form.payment_details
            + "</p>";

htmlBody += "<p>Please quote the order number in your "
            + "correspondence.</p>";

// Send an e-mail to the user.
MailApp.sendEmail({
  to: form.email,
  subject: "Order placed",
  htmlBody: htmlBody
});

htmlBody += "<p> </p>";
htmlBody += '<p>Click <a href="'
            + ScriptApp.getService().getUrl()
            + '?order_number=' + orderNumber
            + '" >here</a> to dispatch the order.</p>';

/*
 * Send an e-mail to the Accounts department with the same
 * content as to the user e-mail, additionally a clickable URL
 * with the order number appended as a query to the published
 * URL.
 *
 */
MailApp.sendEmail({
```

```
    to: "Accounts department email id",
    subject: "Order - " + orderNumber,
    htmlBody: htmlBody
  });

  // Return confirmation message to user.
  return "Order placed successfully and more details " \
        + "has been sent to " + form.email;
};
```

Remember to publish the script again with a new version. Now, the form should look like this:

The sample submitted data in the spreadsheet looks as follows:

	A	B	C	D	E	F	G	H	I	J	K
1	Order #	Item	Unit price	Quantity	Total price	Delivery address	Phone #	Email	Payment details	Shipment details	Delivered on
2	1451855680910	Item 1	4.1	1	4.1			test@example.com			
3	1451863040730	Item 1	4.1	1	4.1			test@example.com			
4	1451863732014	Item 3	3.5	10	35	Delivery ad	1234567890	test@example.c	1234 4567 8912 2345		
5	1451863864679	Item 6	1.1	26	28.6	Delivery ad	1234567890	test@example.c	1234 4567 8912 2345		
6	1451863907071	Item 10	8.6	1	8.6	Delivery ad	1234567890	test@example.com			
7											
8											

Orders ▾ Stock ▾

The sample content of the user e-mail looks as follows:

Order number: 1451875765851

Item: Item 10

Unit price: 8.6

Quantity: 1

Total price: 8.6

Delivery address: Delivery address provided by user

Phone number: 1234567890

Payment details: Payment details provided by user

Please quote order number in your correspondance.

The only difference of the e-mail content to the **Accounts** section is an additional link (which you can see in the sample e-mail content screenshot as follows) of the dispatch form (we will create this form next).

Order number: 1451875765851

Item: Item 10

Unit price: 8.6

Quantity: 1

Total price: 8.6

Delivery address: Delivery address provided by user

Phone number: 1234567890

Payment details: Payment details provided by user

Please quote order number in your correspondance.

Click here to dispatch the order.

Up to this point, what we have set up is:

- The user can submit the Order form
- Script appends the submitted data to the spreadsheet
- Script sends confirmation e-mails both to the user and the **Accounts** department

Creating the dispatch form

As mentioned earlier, we will create the dispatch form now. Create a new HTML file named as `Dispatch` and enter the following code in it:

```html
<!-- Dispatch.html -->
<!DOCTYPE html>
<html>
  <head>
    <base target="_top">
    <link rel="stylesheet"
     href="//ssl.gstatic.com/docs/script/css/add-ons1.css" />
    <script
     src="//ajax.googleapis.com/ajax/libs/jquery/
     1.10.2/jquery.min.js"></script>

    <script>
      // On document load, assign submit function to the submit
      //  button's click event
      $(function(){
        $("#btnSubmit").click(submit);
      });


      function submit(){
        // Remove already displayed messages, if any.
        $("#success,#error").remove();
        this.disabled = true;

        google.script.run
          .withSuccessHandler(function(msg,elem){
            elem.disabled = false;
            showSuccess(msg,elem);
          })
          .withFailureHandler(function(msg, elm){
            elm.disabled = false;
            showError(msg, elm);
          })
          .withUserObject(this)
          .dispatchOrder( this.parentNode );
      }
```

```
        function showSuccess(msg,elm) {
          var span = $('<span id="success">
          <font color="green"> ' + msg + '</font></span>');
          $(elm).after(span);
        }


        function showError(msg,elm) {
          var span = $('<span id="error" class="error"> '
          + msg + '</span>');
          $(elm).after(span);
        }
      </script>
  </head>

  <body>
    <form>
      <table>
        <tr>
        <td><label>Order number:</label></td>
        <td><input name="order_number"
              type="text" readonly value="<?= order[0] ?>" /></td>
        </tr>

        <tr>
        <td><label>Item:</label></td>
        <td><input type="text" readonly
              value="<?= order[1] ?>" /></td>
        </tr>

        <tr>
        <td><label>Quantity:</label></td>
        <td><input type="number" readonly
              value="<?= order[3] ?>" /></td>
        </tr>

        <tr>
        <td><label>Deliver to:</label></td>
        <td><textarea readonly value="<?= order[5] ?>">
              </textarea></td>
        </tr>

        <tr>
        <td><label>Shipment details:</label></td>
```

```
        <td><textarea name="shipment_details"
              placeholder="Enter shipment details." >
              </textarea></td>
        </tr>

        <tr>
        <td><input name="email" type="hidden"
              value="<?= order[7] ?>" /></td>
        </tr>
    </table>

    <br />
    <input class="blue"
      id="btnSubmit" type="button" value="Submit" />
  </form>
 </body>
</html>
```

The script handlers are a subset of the Order form handlers, and most of the HTML elements are read-only, except the shipment details. The dispatch form looks like:

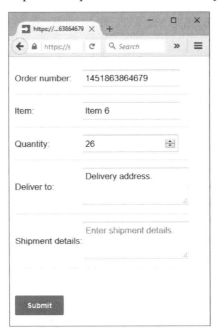

We can use only one doGet function in a script project or web application, but we have to use two forms with the same published URL. How can we open two different forms with the same published URL?

You remember that we appended the order number to the published URL in the `postOrder` handler. An example of the dispatch URL with the order number as a query string will look as follows:

```
https://script.google.com/macros/s/AKfycbwRUVS6z5rjrAw8M-
au9_ICYzixTVB3msLOCmoF5JCBVFNzY_7k/exec?order_number=1451875765851
```

The preceding URL is nothing but the published URL with the order number appended as a query string.

We will update the `doGet` function to parse this query string. If the order number is present, then return the dispatch form; otherwise, return the `Order` form:

```
function doGet(e){
  var orderNumber = e.parameter.order_number;

  if(orderNumber){

    /*
     *   If order number present in query string
     *   then serve dispatch form to order processing unit.
     *
     */
    var template = HtmlService.createTemplateFromFile("Dispatch");
    var data = SheetOrders.getDataRange().getValues();

    for(var i in data){
      if( data[i][0] == orderNumber ){
        template.order = data[i];
        break;
      }
    };

  } else {

    /*
     *   If order number not present in query string
     *   then serve order form to the user.
     *
     */
    var template = HtmlService.createTemplateFromFile("Order");
    template.pricelist = getPrice();
```

```
    };

    var html = template.evaluate();
    return HtmlService.createHtmlOutput(html);
}
```

Now, the doGet function can handle both situations.

Dispatching the articles

As soon as the dispatch person enters the shipment details in the dispatch form and submits it, the script should update the shipment details in the spreadsheet and should send a notification e-mail to the user. So, we will add the dispatchOrder server function to handle these tasks:

```
function dispatchOrder(form){
  // Shipment details column number minus 1.
  const SHIPMENT_DETAILS = 9;

  var orderNumber = form.order_number;
  var deliveryAddress = form.delivery_address;
  var userEmail = form.email;
  var shipmentDetails = form.shipment_details;

  var data = SheetOrders.getDataRange().getValues();

  for(var i = 0; i < data.length; i++){
    if(data[i][0] == orderNumber){
      SheetOrders.getRange(i+1, SHIPMENT_DETAILS+1)
        .setValue(shipmentDetails);

      var htmlBody = "<p>Order number: "
        + orderNumber + " has been dispatched to </p>"
        + "<p>" + deliveryAddress + "</p>"
        + "<p>By " + shipmentDetails + "</p>"
        + "<p> </p>"
        + '<p>Click <a href="' + ScriptApp.getService().getUrl()
        + '?order_number=' + orderNumber
        + '&delivered=true" >here</a> '
        + 'to acknowledge the delivery.</p>';

      // Send email to the user
      MailApp.sendEmail({
        to: userEmail,
```

```
          subject: "Order dispatched",
          htmlBody: htmlBody
      });

      // Return confirmation to the dispatch team.
      return "Shipment details updated and user notified by " \
            + "an e-mail.";
    }
  };

    // Displays error if query order_number not found in sheet.
    throw "Order number not found.";
  };
```

A sample dispatch notification e-mail content is shown here:

Order number: 1451875765851 has been dispatched to

Delivery address provided by user

By Courier name and number

Click here to acknowledge the delivery.

Enabling the user to acknowledge the article delivery

If the user receives the items, then he/she clicks on the link to acknowledge. The same published URL is used this time too with an additional delivered query string.

For example:

```
https://script.google.com/macros/s/AKfycbwaqlj_kBAn9LLav0qv6GmXlWk-
hwIosHA-
1_1YoMutiiuGy84/exec?order_number=1451875765851&delivered=true
```

To handle this query, the doGet function should be updated again as follows:

```
function doGet(e){
   var delivered = e.parameter.delivered;

   if(delivered){
      // If order delivered then just update delivery date.
```

```
  updateDelivery(e);

  // Returning text content is enough, HtmlService not needed.
  return ContentService.createTextOutput("Thank you!");
}

var orderNumber = e.parameter.order_number;

if(orderNumber){

  /*
   *  If order number present in query string
   *  then serve dispatch form to order processing unit.
   *
   */
  var template = HtmlService.createTemplateFromFile("Dispatch");
  var data = SheetOrders.getDataRange().getValues();

  for(var i in data){
    if( data[i][0] == orderNumber ){
      template.order = data[i];
      break;
    }
  };

} else {

  /*
   *  If order number not present in query string
   *  then serve order form to the user.
   *
   */
  var template = HtmlService.createTemplateFromFile("Order");
  template.pricelist = getPrice();

};

var html = template.evaluate();
return HtmlService.createHtmlOutput(html);
}
```

Another handler, the `updateDelivery` function, should be added as follows:

```
function updateDelivery(e){
  // Delivery date column number minus one.
  const DELIVERED_ON = 10;

  var orderNumber = e.parameter.order_number;
  var deliveryDate = new Date();
  var data = SheetOrders.getDataRange().getValues();

  // Update delivery date on matched order number.
  for(var i = 0; i < data.length; i++){
    if(""+data[i][0] == orderNumber){
      SheetOrders.getRange(i+1, DELIVERED_ON+1)
        .setValue(deliveryDate);
    }
  };
}
```

This function updates the current date as the delivered date. A sample spreadsheet with the `Delivered on` column updated is shown as follows:

Congratulations! You have created a full-blown, real-world order processing workflow application.

Summary

In this chapter, you learned and created a useful real-world order processing application. In the next chapter, you will learn to overcome script in maximum execution time and learn to use script code from other script files or libraries including OAuth library. You will also learn to create add-ons.

9

More Tips and Tricks and Creating an Add-on

In the previous chapter, you built an order processing workflow application. In this chapter, you will learn:

- To overcome script maximum execution time restriction
- To use script codes from other script files or libraries
- Create add-ons that use the OAuth2 external library

Overcoming the "script exceeded maximum execution time" error

What if one of your script functions has a bug that causes endless (not terminating) execution, for example, an endless for loop and/or while loop. There are no remedies other than carefully examining the loop terminating statements.

Sometimes, your script may be flawless or bug free, but if it needs to handle a large spreadsheet or external data, it may take a long time to complete the execution. The maximum allowed time for your script to run continuously is 6 minutes. If it exceeds that limit, GAS would throw the "Exceeded maximum execution time" exception.

 For a list of other limitations, please visit: `https://developers. google.com/apps-script/guides/services/quotas#current_ limitations`.

To overcome this bottleneck, you can follow these steps. For example, if your doLengthyProcess function takes a long time to finish, then manually create a minute's trigger for the doLengthyProcess function so that it executes every 10 minutes. Your function should periodically check the elapsed time since the start. If the function completes successfully within the time limit then, at the end of the function, it deletes the trigger. Otherwise, the trigger value is stored in a loop counter in a dedicated Sheet or in script properties. This value should be read and assigned to the loop counter, when the function is triggered again.

A sample skeleton of such a function is given here:

```
var ss = SpreadsheetApp.getActiveSpreadsheet();

// A dedicated sheet to store values temporarily.
var sheet = ss.getSheetByName("Settings");

function doLengthyProcess() {
  // Prefix '+' to get date as epochy number.
  var elapsedTime, startTime = +new Date();

  // Loop variable.
  // Load value of 'i' from spreadsheet cell, or default 0.
  var i = sheet.getRange("A1").getValue() || 0;

  for(; i<1000; i++){
    // Your time consuming process goes here.
    ...
    ...
    ...
    ...

    // Recalculate elapsedTime.
    elapsedTime = +new Date() - startTime;

    if(elapsedTime> 300000){ // 300000 ms or 5 minutes.
      sheet.getRange("A1").setValue(i);
      return;
    }
  };

  // Loop completed successfully, so delete trigger.
  deleteTriggers_();
}
```

```
// Helper function
function deleteTriggers_(){
  var triggers = ScriptApp.getProjectTriggers();
  triggers.forEach(function(trigger){
    ScriptApp.deleteTrigger(trigger);
    /*
      * Wait a moment before calling deleteTrigger again.
      * Otherwise you may get warning message something like
      * "Service invoked too many times..."
      *
      */
    Utilities.sleep(1000); // In millisecond.
  });

};
```

To sum up, you create an "every minutes" trigger manually, and then the function executes until it completes successfully.

If you feel hesitant to create triggers manually, you can create them by script as we discussed in *Chapter 3, Parsing and Sending E-mails* but this time, create every minute's trigger:

```
function createTrigger_(funcName,minutes){
// Delete already created triggers if any.
deleteTriggers_();
  ScriptApp.newTrigger(funcName).timeBased()
    .everyMinutes(minutes).create();
}
```

Here you created a trigger for the functions which do not start immediately but with a delay. However, if you want to automate everything, it means creating a trigger and calling the function immediately. Create another function `startProcess` as shown here:

```
function startProcess(){
  createTrigger_("doLengthyProcess",10);
  doLengthyProcess();
}
```

Now, you just need to run the `startProcess` function. Also, you can assign a menu for this function.

Configuring your script project to use external libraries

Sometimes you would like to reuse code from other script project(s) or other programmer's code in your projects. You can import external code as it resides in the current project. You need to make a simple configuration in your current project.

For an example, we will explain how to import the previous chapter's code into the current project.

1. Open any one of your previously created scripts (for example, *Chapter 8, Building a Workflow Application*) in the script editor, save a version if you haven't already.

2. Now, click on the **File** menu and then **Project properties**. The **Project properties** dialog will open as shown here:

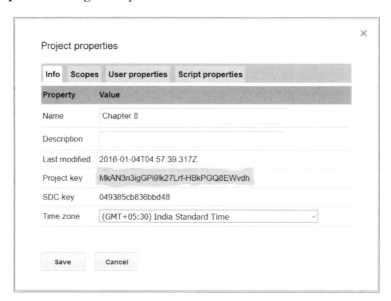

3. Copy the **Project key** value (this value should be different for your project).

4. Open the current script, navigate to **Resources | Libraries...**, and then the **Included Libraries** dialog will open as shown here:

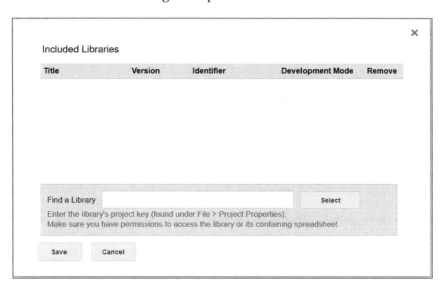

5. Paste **Project key** (you already copied in step 1) into the **Find a Library** textbox and click on the **Select** button.

Now, the Chapter 8 project will be included in the libraries list as shown here:

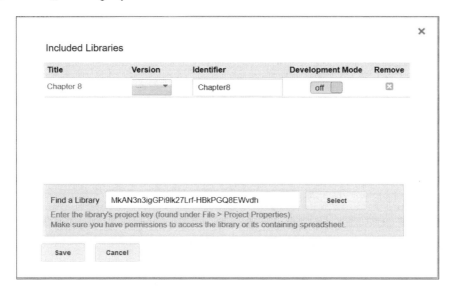

Select the version (the version you are going to use in this current project); and if you like, you can change the identifier (Chapter8) too. Leave **Development Mode** off means using a selected version; set it to **on** to override the selected version and use the current version. Click on the **Save** button to save the changes.

Now all the functions (except private functions, that is, function names appended with "_") and the global variables are available to use in the current project. For example, you can use the doGet function from *Chapter 8, Building a Workflow Application* here by prefixing with the identifier. It means that you can use the doGet function as Chapter8.doGet(), the getPrice function as Chapter8.getPrice(), and so on.

If you need more explanation, then here is a sample usage:

```
function test(){

  var pricelist = Chapter8.getPrice();

  Logger.log(pricelist);
}
```

Using JSDoc annotations

In the preceding test function, you can see that the code hint became active as soon as you type a '.' next to the identifier name (Chapter8). This shows all the functions and global variables available in the external library as shown here:

The preceding code hints are generic, for example, index shown as Object. For detailed code hints, you should use the JSDoc style documentations (annotations or comments at top lines of function definitions).

For example, if you used the following annotations to the getPrice function in *Chapter 8, Building a Workflow Application*:

```
/**
 *   Returns price list data from the Stock tab/sheet
 *
 *   @param {number} index
 *   @return {array}
 *
 */
function getPrice(index){
        ...
}
```

Then the code hint would be as shown here:

```
* Code.gs ×

function test(){
  var pricelist = Chapter8.|

  Logger.log(pricelist);      SheetOrders : Object

}                             SheetStock : Object

                              dispatchOrder(Object form) : void

                              doGet(Object e) : void

                              getPrice(number index) : array

                              postOrder(Object form) : void

                              ss : Object

                              updateDelivery(Object e) : void
```

Now, you can notice how the code hint returns with useful information for the getPrice function.

For further reading on JSDoc, visit: `https://developers.google.com/closure/compiler/docs/js-for-compiler`.

Using the OAuth open source library

If your application interacts with external libraries other than Google's basic services, then it should be authenticated. In other words, if your application runs on behalf of a user, then that user should authorize your application to grant access to his/her data. GAS does not provide any built-in authentication service, but you can use an open source OAuth library.

Creating, testing, and publishing add-ons

If you need to use other external libraries in your current project, you need to know the project key and you should have at least read access to that project. At the same time, every new version of the master project will not reflect in the client project unless the client selects the current version. Add-ons override this configuration hassle.

Add-ons are installable scripts by the click of a button, no configuration required. You can install add-ons in Sheets, Docs, and/or Forms published by the other programmer or from the Google Chrome Web Store.

Installing add-ons from Chrome Web Store

To install an add-on from Chrome Web Store, open the document (Sheets, Docs, or Forms) and click on **Get add-ons...** from the **Add-ons** menu. Select any one of your favorite add-ons from the **Add-ons** dialog (if you hover your mouse over any add-on, then a plus symbol will appear on the application; click on it and authorize if required). A sample **Add-ons** dialog is shown here, but the actual add-ons included may vary from time to time.

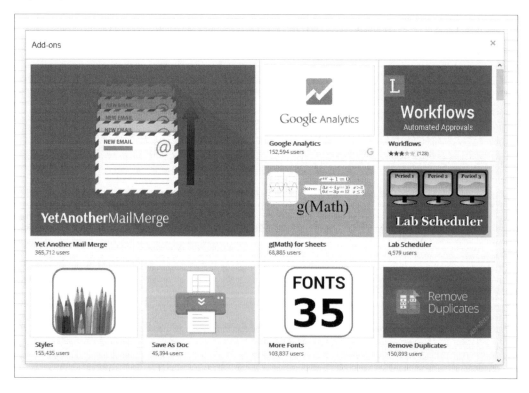

You will get that add-on installed and added to your document's **Add-ons** menu. Each add-on comes with easy-to-use menu items. For example, if you installed **autoCrat** then the menu item would look like in the screenshot shown here:

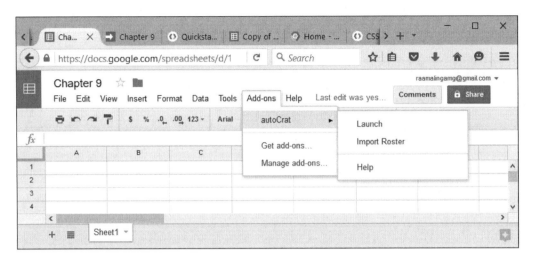

Creating custom add-ons

You can create add-ons by yourself, use within your other documents, or share with other users. Your users can use your add-ons but cannot see the code. So, you can keep your intellectual property (that is, code and data) confidential.

Add menu items to the **Add-on** menu such that:

```
function onOpen(e){
  SpreadsheetApp.getUi().createAddonMenu()
  .addItem("Show Sidebar", "showSidebar")
  .addToUi();
}
```

The addItem method's first argument is the label for the menu item and the next one is the function name. Add the onInstall event function if you are going to publish an add-on for Chrome Web Store such that:

```
function onInstall(e){
  onOpen(e);
}
```

The preceding function invokes the `onOpen` function while the add-on is installed for the first time in Sheets, Docs, or Forms. If your add-on needs a user interface, then create the sidebar dialog:

```
/**
 *  Opens sidebar in the document containing the add-on's
 *   user interface.
 *
 */
function showSidebar() {
  SpreadsheetApp.getUi().showSidebar(
    HtmlService.createHtmlOutputFromFile('Sidebar')
  );
}
```

To style the sidebar (create `Sidebar.html`), you can use the officially supported CSS package from the `https://ssl.gstatic.com/docs/script/css/add-ons1.css` URL.

 For more help on this package visit `https://developers.google.com/apps-script/add-ons/css`.

Testing your add-on

To test your add-on within the script editor, navigate to the **Publish | Test as add-on...** menu and then within the resulting dialog select the document in which you want to test the add-on as shown here:

To share your add-on with others, it is enough to share the document. More than that, if you would like to publish the script, follow the **Publish | Deploy** as an add-on menu. In the resulting dialog, fill the required fields and follow the guidelines provided. Your add-on should strictly adhere to the Chrome Web Store's content and style guidelines and undergo a review process before being listed and made available to the public.

 For more information on add-ons, visit `https://developers.` `google.com/apps-script/add-ons/`.

Creating an add-on that uses an OAuth2 external library

To get hands-on experience on all aforesaid concepts, we will create an add-on that can send an active spreadsheet as a PDF attachment to the active user's e-mail ID.

Create a new script project in Sheets. In the script editor, we will first create a few global variables as shown here:

```
var ss = SpreadsheetApp.getActiveSpreadsheet();
var activeSheet = ss.getActiveSheet();
var activeSheetName = activeSheet.getSheetName();
```

Next, take a look at the onOpen and onInstall trigger functions.

```
/**
 * Creates a menu entry in the Google Sheets UI when the document
 * is opened.
 *
 * @param {object} e The event parameter for a simple onOpen
 * trigger.
 *
 */
function onOpen(e){
  // Create an Add-on menu item and associate a function.
  SpreadsheetApp.getUi().createAddonMenu()
  .addItem("Sheet To PDF", "sendSheetAsPdfToActiveUser")
  .addToUi();
}
```

```
/**
 * Runs when the add-on is installed.
 *
 * @param {object} e The event parameter for a simple onInstall
 * trigger.
 *
 */
function onInstall(e){
  onOpen(e);
}
```

In the onOpen trigger, we have associated the function sendSheetAsPdfToActiveUser to the **Sheet To PDF** menu item. We will create that function now:

```
/**
 * Sends PDF attachment to the active user e-mail id.
 *
 */
function sendSheetAsPdfToActiveUser(){
  // Get active user's email id.
  var mailTo = Session.getActiveUser().getEmail();
  // Returns either pdf or false.
  var attachments = getAttachments();
  // Send only if there is attachment.
  if(attachments){
    MailApp.sendEmail(
        mailTo, activeSheetName, '', {attachments:attachments}
  );
    }
}
```

The said function sends an e-mail with the PDF attachment, which is returned from the getAttachments function. An example is given here:

```
/**
 * Authorizes the application for the first time or the token
 *   expires. If authentication token is valid then returns the pdf
 *   file with other attachment parameter otherwise prompts the
 *   user to authorize.
 *
 *   @return {Object} Array of attachment objects.
 */
```

```
function getAttachments(){
  // Authenticated service object.
  var service = getGoogleService();

  // Proceed further only if authenticated, otherwise prompt for
  // authentication.
  if (service.hasAccess()) {

    // The url to download activesheet as pdf.
    var url = ss.getUrl()
        .replace("edit", "export?gid=" + activeSheet.getSheetId()
          + "&format=pdf&attachment=false");

    // The access token should be sent on every request.
    var headers = {
        Authorization:'Bearer ' + service.getAccessToken()
    };

    // Send request to the pdf url with the access token.
    var response = UrlFetchApp.fetch(url, { headers:headers });

    // Returned content.
    var content = response.getContent();

    // Returns as an array of objects.
    return [{
      fileName: activeSheetName + ".pdf",
      content: content,
      mimeType:"application/pdf"
    }];

  } else {

    // Authorization url from the service object.
    var authorizationUrl = service.getAuthorizationUrl();

    // Side bar with the authorization link.
var template = HtmlService
    .createTemplate(
    '<a href="<?= authorizationUrl ?>"
    target="_blank">Authorize</a>.'
);
```

```
      // Authorization url assigned to template
      template.authorizationUrl = authorizationUrl;

      // Finally evaluate the template and show sidebar.
      var page = template.evaluate();
      SpreadsheetApp.getUi().showSidebar(page);

      // Attracting user attention.
      Browser.msgBox('Authorize on sidebar and run again.');

      // Return false, so no need to send e-mail.
      return false;
   }
}
```

The said function prompts the user to authenticate the application if he is using it for the first time or already has an authenticated token but it is expired. If the authenticated token is valid, then it returns the PDF attachment, otherwise it returns false.

Now, the only thing we have left to do is implementing OAuth2 flow. We will create a function for the same:

```
/**
 * Executes OAuth2 flow.
 *
 * @return {Object} Authentication service object.
 *
 */
function getGoogleService(){
  /*
   * Create a new service with the given name (here 'PACKT').
   * The name will be used when persisting the authorized token,
   * so ensure it is unique within the scope of the property
   * store.
   *
   */
  return OAuth2.createService("PACKT")

// Endpoint URLs are same for all Google services.
.setAuthorizationBaseUrl(
'https://accounts.google.com/o/oauth2/auth'
)
.setTokenUrl('https://accounts.google.com/o/oauth2/token')
```

```
  /*
   * Replace with your client ID and secret got from developers
   * console.
   *
   */
  .setClientId('...')
  .setClientSecret('...')

  // A callback function to complete the OAuth2 flow.
  .setCallbackFunction('authCallback')

  // A place to store authenticated tokens.
  .setPropertyStore(PropertiesService.getUserProperties())

  /*
   * Scopes to request, separate with space if more than one
   * scope.
   *
   */
  .setScope('https://docs.google.com/feeds/')


  /*
   * Google-specific parameters.
   *
   * Sets the login hint, which will prevent the account chooser
   * screen from being shown to users if logged in with multiple
   * accounts.
   *
   */
  .setParam('login_hint', Session.getActiveUser().getEmail())

  // Requests offline access.
  .setParam('access_type', 'offline')

  /*
   * Forces the approval prompt every time to show up.
   * This is useful for testing, but not desirable in a production
   * application.
   *
   */
  .setParam('approval_prompt', 'force');
}
```

Don't forget to replace your own client ID and secret. We will see how to get them. Can you remember what you did to enable advanced services in *Chapter 5, Creating Google Calendar and Drive Applications*? Use the same steps here, but with a few additional tasks.

Within the script editor, navigate to **Resources | Developers Console Project...** and click on **View Developers Console** on the dialog that opens:

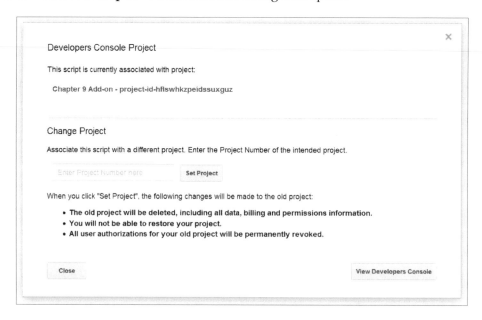

That should take you to the developer's console dashboard where you can click on the **Enable and manage APIs** option.

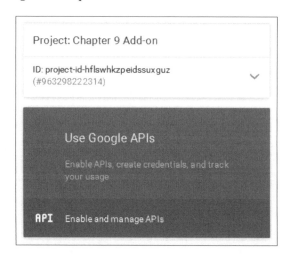

Once enabled, click on **Credentials** on the left pane of the console dashboard:

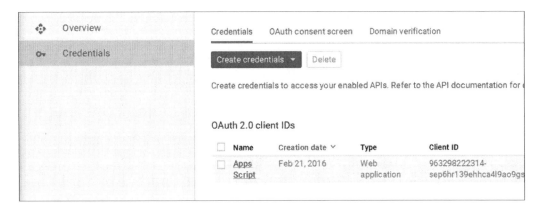

To complete the OAuth2 flow, this callback function will be invoked, and it shows a message to the user. Then, the OAuth2 client IDs are listed as **Apps Script**. Click on **Apps Script** to see the details as shown here:

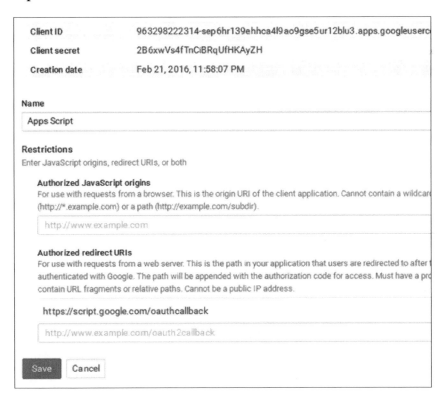

You need to add an authorized redirect URL for this project. Enter the URL as shown here, but replaced with your project key:

```
https://script.google.com/macros/d/[[PROJECT KEY]]/usercallback
```

Before clicking on **Save**, a copy of the client ID and client secret is required in the `getGoogleService` function. Once this is done, click on **Save**; you can return to this dashboard anytime afterwards.

Also add the `authCallback` function as shown here:

```
function authCallback(request) {
  var service = getGoogleService();
  var isAuthorized = service.handleCallback(request);

  if (isAuthorized) {
return HtmlService
  .createHtmlOutput('Success! You can close this tab.');
  } else {
return HtmlService
  .createHtmlOutput('Denied. You can close this tab');
  }
}
```

Before testing the add-on, import the OAuth2 client library using the project key:

```
MswhXl8fVhTFUH_Q3UOJbXvxhMjh3Sh48
```

The following are some sample keys:

- OAuth1 Lib Key: `Mb2Vpd5nfD3Pz-_a-39Q4VfxhMjh3Sh48`
- OAuth2 Lib Key: `MswhXl8fVhTFUH_Q3UOJbXvxhMjh3Sh48`

For more information on open source OAuth2 external library, visit `https://github.com/googlesamples/apps-script-oauth2`.

Now, you have completed all the setup steps. Refresh the spreadsheet window so that your add-on appears in an **Add-on** menu.

In addition, once authenticated, you can reset or revoke the authentication using this function:

```
function clearService(){
  OAuth2.createService('PACKT')
  .setPropertyStore(PropertiesService.getUserProperties())
  .reset();
}
```

Notice the same service name (PACKT) used here.

Other useful links

- Tutorials: `https://developers.google.com/apps-script/articles`

- Documentation: `https://developers.google.com/apps-script/`

- Blog: `http://googleappsdeveloper.blogspot.in/search/label/Apps%20Script`

Summary

In this chapter, you learned how to overcome script maximum run time restrictions, how to import external libraries, how to use OAuth, and how to create an add-on. We hope you enjoyed reading this book, learning, and gathering hands-on skills on most aspects of the Google Apps Script. Happy coding and enjoy!

Index

D

data, Google Sheets
  reading 35
  writing 35
dispatch form
  creating 183-186
document reviewing application
  creating 131-140
DriveApp class
  about 95
  customized PDF files, creating 95-98
  Drive file routing application,
      creating 98, 99
  Drive file search application,
      creating 100-103
  URL 95

E

e-mail merger application
  building 50-53
e-mails
  inline image, embedding 50
  notification, sending on Form
      submission 44, 45
  sending, with MailApp service 44
  with attachments, sending 49
  with specific keywords in
      message body, forwarding 48
employee timesheet application
  creating 155-165
e-voting application
  creating 72-75
external libraries
  using, by script project
      configuration 194-196

F

file upload application
  creating 152-155
Form
  creating, HtmlService used 63-70
  creating, script used 55-60

Form submission
  e-mail notification, sending on 44-46

G

getSheets() method 34
getValue method 35
getValues method 35
Gmail
  about 4, 5
  attachments, downloading to
      Google Drive 41-44
Gmail Contacts, by script
  creating 33, 34
Gmail Contact search application
  building 35-40
Gmail parser application
  building 40
Google Applications 1, 2
Google Apps Script (GAS)
  about 2, 17
  advantages 3
  limitations 3
  platform-independent 3
  using 5
  version-independent 3
  Visual Basic for Applications (VBA) 2, 3
Google Apps services
  about 6
  Google Sheets, creating 7
Google Calendar 6
Google Cloud 2
Google Docs 6
Google Drive
  about 3, 4
  advantages 3
  Gmail attachments, downloading to 41-44
  Google Sheets, creating 7, 8
Google Forms
  about 14
  creating, within Google Sheets 14
  research 15
Google search application
  creating 108, 109

Google Sheet data
  converting, as PDF file 146-148
  rendering, as HTML with web
    app 142, 143
Google Sheets
  about 6
  accessing 34, 35
  configuring 169-171
  creating, in Google Drive 7, 8
  custom formula, creating 12, 13
  data, reading 35
  data, writing 35
  Google Forms, creating 14
  new projects, creating 11, 12
  sharing 7, 8
  URL 7
Google Translate service
  supported languages, URL 122

H

HtmlService
  defining 62
  used, for creating Form 63-70
HTTP/HTTPS request
  sending, with query string 148-150

I

inline commenting application
  creating 131-140
inline image
  embedding, in e-mail message 50

J

JSDoc annotations
  reference link 197
  using 196, 197
JSON
  returning, by creating web app 144, 145

L

LanguageApp class
  about 121
  language translator application,
    creating 122-131

language translator application
  creating 122-131
Last Traded Price (LTP) 111
limitations
  reference link 191

M

MailApp service
  used, for sending e-mails 44
modal dialog
  creating 27
modeless dialog
  creating 28

O

OAuth open source library
  using 197
offset
  accessing 34, 35
Order form
  creating 171-174
  enhancing 174-182
**order processing workflow application,
    building**
  articles, dispatching 187, 188
  dispatch form, creating 183-186
  Google Sheets, configuring 169-171
  Order form, creating 171-174
  Order form, enhancing 174-182
  steps 168

P

PDF file
  Google Sheet data, converting as 146-148
private functions 42
properties service 41

Q

query string
  HTTP/HTTPS request, sending
    with 148-150

R

range
  accessing 34, 35
Rich Site Summary (RSS)
  about 115
  feed document, skeleton 116
  reader application, creating 117, 118
RSS feed
  creating, ContentService used 150
  document, skeleton 116
RSS reader application
  creating 117, 118

S

script
  debugging 28-31
  publishing, as web application 60-62
  used, for creating Forms 55-60
script exceeded maximum execution time error
  overcoming 191-193
scriptlets 63
script projects
  about 9
  configuration, for using external libraries 194-196
  creating, in Google Sheets 11, 12
  custom formula, creating in Google Sheets 12, 13
  standalone script projects, creating 9, 10
sidebar
  creating 24
stock quote ticker application
  creating 110-112

T

templates 63
throw keyword 158
ticket reservation application
  creating 76-80

toast

  displaying, on button click 22
triggers
  creating, manually 46
  reference link 47
triggers by script
  creating 47, 48
  deleting 47, 48

U

UrlFetchApp class
  about 105-107
  Bitcoin quotes, logging 113
  fetch method 105
  Google search application, creating 108, 109
  optional parameters, using with 121
  stock quote ticker application, creating 110-112
user
  enabling, for article delivery acknowledgments 188-190

V

Visual Basic for Applications (VBA)
  about 2, 3
  advantages 3
  platform-independent 3
  version-independent 3

W

web app
  creating, for rendering Google Sheet data as HTML 142, 143
  creating, to return JSON 144, 145
web application
  script, publishing as 60-62